Through the Morning Fog

Jennifer Malech

WRITTEN IN HONOR OF HENRY MOORE

AUTHOR'S NOTE

In her book, Come Matter Here, Hannah Brencher writes, "There was a time when I thought this book might never exist. Turns out, I had to live the story well before I ever sat down to write it."

When I first wrote this book in 2017, I was going through a very difficult season. There were so many people who prayed with me and believed with me for a miracle during that time. For two years, I waited and trusted God. At times, I felt like none of my prayers were being heard, especially when the situation got worst, but that's when I realized I can't trust my feelings, but must continually lean on God's truth. It is His Word alone that carried me through the foggiest of mornings and continually pointed me towards the hope that is in Christ alone. And, it is there, during the darkest of mornings, that this book was birthed.

During that time, when my heart was hurting in unspeakable ways, these chapters began to spill out as God revealed to me that joy isn't based on our circumstances, but that instead, through the gift of the Holy Spirit, we have full access to joy.

I want to share with all of you the beautiful lessons that God taught me through one of the darkest, yet most solidifying seasons in my life. While I have just recently walked out of the fog and into the light, I wanted to re-visit these chapters.

This book is an invitation, an invitation to take a deep breath and be still and know that God is good. I want this book to feel like you and I are sitting on my front porch (if I had one), a time for us to take in the morning sunrise over a cup of coffee and thank God for another beautiful day. Even when I was walking through a very difficult few years, where my emotional and physical health were in jeopardy due to the difficult family situation I was having to walk through, I started off every single morning thanking God for the gift of another day. I am convinced that gratitude is medicine for the soul. So, today, I hope we start off the day with gratitude in our hearts for the breath in our lungs and the choice to be loved and known by God as we find beauty in the everlasting truth of God's Word.

This is the second version of this devotional, because it turns out I had to live my story well before I ever sat down to re-write these words. But, also, this is the second version because I accidentally deleted the original manuscript. That is a story for another day.

Cheers,
Jennifer

CONTENTS

INTRODUCTION

Have you ever woken to a sunny morning that puts a big smile on your face, but then the next morning, you are suddenly scrambling through your closet trying to find the misplaced umbrella that suddenly needs your attention? Growing up in the Bay Area, I became quite familiar with this sensation. There were some mornings where the fog was so thick that it became terribly difficult to see. And, you didn't know when it would happen. Some mornings were foggy, some were not. Sometimes, it caught you by surprise. And, isn't that just like life? We sigh as the gloom surrounding us has us staring longingly at our sunglasses that now sit atop our car dashboard. How could it be that just yesterday, with the windows rolled down and the sunshine seeping through my skin, I was singing a cheerful tune to *It's Another Day of Sun?*

There are two definitions for the word fog. Find any Merriam Webster's Dictionary that might still be lying around your home and you will find these definitions for yourself.

1. a thick cloud of tiny water droplets suspended in the atmosphere at or near the earth's surface that obscures or restricts visibility

2. something that obscures and confuses a situation or someone's thought processes

Sometimes, and maybe more often than others, fog creeps into our lives and blinds us from where we once stood on a sunny morning. Everything that once seemed certain suddenly becomes uncertain. Through the questions, doubts, and confusion, your thoughts are going about a million miles per hour as you find it difficult to put one foot in front of the other. You would rather be stuck in traffic singing *It's Another Day of Sun* than going through the fog of life's current circumstances.

If each of us shared our stories with one another, I am certain that we would begin to see that none of us have been spared from difficult chapters. That is the reality of life. Thus, it is for this reason that we must build a strong foundation for our lives-a firm faith that is unwavering, no matter what life looks like outside your window today. The fog is guaranteed. And, sometimes, the fog is necessary. It is in these moments, on the foggiest of days, that you learn to trust God in a way that you wouldn't have otherwise. My dear friend, Lauren, once told me that if we didn't go through trials or pain, then our faith would be solely theoretical. I couldn't agree more.

While you may not be able to see what's in front of you right now, just hold on. Put your daily trust in God's Word. True faith is trusting when you cannot see what lies ahead, when the impossible seems it will never become possible. True faith is putting our hope in the One who holds it all together.

One of my favorite scriptures that I have taped to my bathroom mirror is 2 Corinthians 4:18. It is a reminder for me to daily live my life fixated on Jesus and our Kingdom assignment while we are here on earth, for however long that may be.

"So we fix our eyes not on what is seen, but on what is unseen, since what is seen is temporary, but what is unseen is eternal."

When we live our lives with an eternal perspective, a perspective that understands that this earth is just our temporary home, then we will live with a passion that knows that our ultimate purpose is to share God's love through the light of the gospel with those around us, no matter how difficult our own circumstances might be. Let God use your pain as a lighthouse on the foggiest of mornings. It will not only lead you home, but it might be the very thing that will lead others there, too. And, if you are having a hard time keeping your eyes lifted, my hope is that these words can be the voice of someone standing in the gap for you, to give you a faith boost, and remind you that you are not ever for one moment alone. As you read the stories in this book, my prayer is that God would meet you right where you are. My hope is that you and I would daily allow our lives to be transformed by the Word of God and understand that the most important part of our lives is our daily devotion with Him. Through the thick and thin, He is the only One who can give us what we are searching for. Psalm 34:18-19 states, "God is close to the brokenhearted and saves those who are crushed in spirit. The righteous person may have many troubles, but the Lord delivers him from them all."

This devotional is filled with 30 Days of Scriptures and encouragement to trust God through the morning fog. You can either read it day by day, or all in one sitting. Whichever way you choose, all I want you to know is that with God by your side, you've got this, friend.

JENNIFER MALECH

1

GOD IS IN THE UNSEEN

"We do not need more intellectual power, we need more spiritual power. We do not need more of the things that are seen, we need more of the things that are unseen."
-Calvin Coolidge

As the ocean's turquoise colored waves danced together in the wake of the morning sun, I was overwhelmed by the vast ocean as I so very often am when I go for runs along the beach. I grew up in the Monterey Bay Area and absolutely loved waking up early to run alongside the cliffs, soothed by the sounds of the roaring waves and the seagull's morning greeting. There is something so magnificent about the ocean, the ways in which the waves just come and go, and bring forth both feelings of power and peace at the same time. The ocean is my favorite wonder of nature. It makes me terribly sad to think that there are those who have never seen the ocean with their own eyes. If I could give you a gift today, it would be a gift to the seaside. So, although we may not be able to go on a morning run alongside the ocean right now, I want to take you there for a moment.

One of my favorite places in all the earth is Point Lobos, a

State Park just outside Carmel, California. Look it up. Better yet, add it to your bucket list. I promise you that it will be worth it. In my opinion, Point Lobos is the best place for a morning run or walk. Whenever I would go home for the holidays, after having moved to Southern California, I would always add a morning run at Point Lobos to my itinerary. From anywhere in the park, you can hear the roar of the ocean waves. The trails take you through the Monterey Pine trees, the green moss dangling from the branches, guiding you towards the powerful sound of the ocean. You pick up your pace, enjoying the beauty of the rugged trails, but growing in anticipation for that first glimpse of the ocean. And, then, just beyond the clearing of the woods, the glory of the cliffsides display a scene that looks as though you just entered a different world.

In the back of my mind, I can hear the words from one of my favorite Sleeping at Last songs, Saturn. *"With shortness of breath, I'll explain the infinite. How rare and beautiful it truly is that we exist."* If you ever do find yourself in Point Lobos or beautiful Big Sur, listen to Sleeping at Last's album, Atlas, while you walk along those cliffsides, gazing at the mystery of the Pacific Ocean. It's a magical experience. You'll find a stillness and peace that is so refreshing and wonderful, you'll never want to leave.

I painted this picture to help you understand the concept of trusting God with the unknown, with that which we cannot see. I believe that God placed this restlessness inside of us that draws us to His love, like the anticipation I felt as I ran through the woods, hearing the draw of the ocean, even if I could not see it with my own eyes just yet, at least not until I made it through the clearing.

There are so many times in our lives when we are placed in situations that we cannot see what lies ahead, and it terrifies us, almost as much as the power of the ocean's waves. The unknown is something that none of us ever get comfortable with, and making peace with the unknown requires us to trust in the One who knows beginning to end, the One who truly does work all things together for His good.

When we can't see what lies ahead, we have to place our trust in something that is more than us, something that is more magnificent than any natural wonder here on earth. **We may not be able to see God, but due to our experiences, our experiences of His presence and the unchanging Word of God, we have proof that He is present in our unseen and is working on our behalf.** And, let me clarify for a moment. We do not put our confidence in God because of our experiences, but we trust in God because His Word remains constant through all of time. When our eyes first glimpse the ocean's horizon, our naked eye cannot see from first glimpse the sea life that is underneath it, but if we dive a little deeper, we will find a whole new world that we can believe in. The ocean is 32,000 ft deep. To give you a deeper understanding, the ocean is a little over six miles deep. There are places in the ocean that we will never be able to go to, but God sees it all. When I gaze at the ocean, all I can see is the sea otters that are eating their morning breakfast atop the water or the occasional dolphin that surfs the ocean's edge. Yet, because of my faith and my own snorkeling adventures in Hawaii, I know that there   is   life   beyond   the   shores.

When I can't see beneath the surface of my circumstances, I remind myself of where God has brought me from. I remind myself of what God has done, not only for me, but for His people throughout all of history. As we study the Word, we undeniably come to the revelation that God is in control. 2 Corinthians 5:17 states, "For we walk by faith, not by sight."

God is asking us to trust Him beyond what we can see. There's so much more to what meets the naked eye. Just as God takes care of the ocean and the sea life that many of us will never uncover during our time here on earth, He takes care of you and I. He sees the trails that lie ahead in our lives, and knows what will not only be the best path for us, but what will ultimately bring glory to His Name. When we live our lives with eternity in mind, we will begin to understand that it doesn't matter what comes next, because ultimately, His glory will be revealed.

2

HAPPINESS IS TEMPORARY, JOY IS ETERNAL

"The fact that our heart yearns for something that earth can't supply is proof that heaven is our home."
-C.S. Lewis

"One drop of the Lord's mercy is better than an ocean of the world's temporary comforts."
-Lysa Terkeurst

I love to travel. Actually, that's an understatement. I adore traveling. I become more alive when I travel, as though there are parts of me that I never knew existed until I step into a new city or country. There is nothing more eye-opening than traveling to a culture that is far different from your own.

Some of my favorite adventures have included a road trip to the English countryside, going on a four-day trek through the Andes Mountains of Peru, eating pizza along Italy's Amalfi Coast for a Thanksgiving I will never forget, and wandering the streets of Barcelona's Gothic Quarter, just to name a few.

While taking a morning stroll through Barcelona last

summer, I went into a café and ordered myself a cappuccino, my favorite morning drink. Really, though. Is there anything better than drinking a cappuccino in Europe? Okay, a croissant would have made it better, but I ordered the avocado toast on the menu. Yes, I was the typical California girl needing her daily dose of avocado across seas. Anyways, when I sat down, I pulled out my phone and wrote these words, "Travel is a change of pace, it's listening to several languages all around you, it's all five senses heightened to the unfamiliar, and it's roaming the streets with no particular destination." There is something about traveling that gives me the happiest of butterflies in my stomach as my worldview is broadened and my photo gallery is filled with sights and wonders that will never escape my memory. You become a new person when you travel. You'll never be the same when you've walked on new roads and experienced cultures that are far different from your own. The fact is that we can learn so much from one another and one another's cultures, even within our own country. And, as much as I love traveling, there is something else that also happens whenever I travel. I come to realize all the more that the temporary pleasure of travel will never fulfill me. Happiness is a temporary feeling. As I sat in a café in Barcelona, sipping on the perfect cappuccino, I realized that one day, all of this will fade away. This is our temporary home.

What are our lives without Jesus? We strive for happiness, and reach inwards trying to find it, but come to discover that it is only by reaching upwards towards heaven that we will find life's greatest gift: joy. Because the truth of the matter is, when you have gone through some very difficult and unexpected trials in life, there is a feeling that grips your throat that could care less about travel, food, and beautiful songs and places. There is a yearning inside of you for something that goes beyond the temporary, a draw to something that is certain, a return to the truth that God reveals in His word to you and I. 1 Peter 1:8-9 reveals, "Though you have not seen Him, you love Him; and even though you do not see Him now, you believe in Him and are filled with an inexpressible and glorious joy for you are receiving the end result of your faith, the salvation of your souls." Salvation, the greatest gift and the message of the gospel, can fill our lungs with inexpressible joy. If there is anything that I have learned, it is that happiness and joy are two entirely different things. Happiness is temporary, joy is eternal. This is why, when life's circumstances have filled our lungs with sadness, there is a joy that we can still experience because of the hope that is found in Christ alone. Hebrews 6:19 reminds us, "This hope we have as an anchor of the soul, both sure and steadfast."

Happiness is a gift that we get to experience in this life, and while I am so thankful for wonderful opportunities and experiences here in this life, the things we enjoy here on earth will not satisfy the longing deep within. No matter how many countries I travel to, it will not satisfy my soul. C.S. Lewis once said, "If we find ourselves with a desire that nothing in this world can satisfy, the most probable explanation is that we were made for another world." True joy in this life isn't found in our circumstances or our experiences, but in the rest and the hope that God faithfully walks beside us and that one day, we will get to spend forever with Him in our eternal home. Family, relationships, careers, vacations, money, degrees, achievements, they all come and go. They are fleeting moments of temporary pleasure that will never offer what only His love alone   can   do.
I have found myself at times in desperate situations, where the only thing that could fill me up with joy and give me hope was the unfailing love of Jesus. Whether your world is sunshine and palm trees in paradise or dark clouds and rain in a desert today, we must understand that our true source of joy is found in Christ alone. Every morning, we get to wake up and call on the name of Jesus. Don't take that for granted, friend. Even on the happiest of days and the grandest of adventures, none of it is in comparison to the love of Jesus. It is our source of life, the water that will make us never thirst again. There is nothing else on this earth that can fill you like God's love.

In his book, The Problem of Pain, C.S. Lewis writes, "Don't let your happiness depend on something you may lose." God's love, the most certain thing and the only true promise that we have of never losing, is the only thing that will give the human heart what it longs for.

3

DELIVERANCE COMES BEFORE THE PROMISE

"God's promises are all on condition of humble obedience."
-Ellen G. White

"If God is sending you to a new place, He's sending you with a promise of blessing."
-Kristen Strong

"I promise things will get better." How often have you heard that phrase? Whether it came from a parent, a friend, or a spiritual mentor trying to encourage you through a rough patch, we've all heard these words before. It's supposed to be reassuring, but at times, I wanted to look back at the person who sat across from me and reply with, "But, you don't know that. You can't be certain that things will get better." While this is true, since none of us know what comes next, there is also truth in the Scriptures that points us towards the hope that things will get better. They may not happen in our timing or even happen during our time here on earth, but things will get better, because one day, deliverance will come. We may never understand this side of heaven why things are the way they are, but we can be rest assured that whether it is in this life or the next, God's promise will come to pass. Victory is ours.

How do I know this? 1 John 4:4 states, "You are of God, little children, and have overcome them, because He who is in you is greater than he who is in the world."

To convey this concept, there's a story in the Book of Joshua that I absolutely love. It is the story of Joshua leading the Israelites into the promised land. Read all about it in the first twenty-four chapters of Joshua. It's such a powerful story. One aspect of the story that has always stood out to me above the rest is the part when the Israelites finally reach the new land, that moment when the promise came to fruition. When they crossed over into the Promised Land, the Jordan River covers up the dry land that they had been walking on. In Joshua 4:22-24, it states, "then you shall let your children know, saying, 'Israel crossed over this Jordan on dry land'; for the LORD your God dried up the waters of the Jordan before you until you had crossed over, as the LORD your God did to the Red Sea, which He dried up before us until we had crossed over, that all the peoples of the earth may know the hand of the LORD, that it *is* mighty, that you may fear the LORD your God forever."

When God delivers us into a promise that He has placed over our lives and we learn to trust Him and gain reverence for Him, God will cover up/close the places that we had once been in so that there is no possible way of return. You can't receive the promise without first receiving deliverance. Deliverance comes from obedience.

In this season of life, wherever you are, the Israelites deliverance into the Promised Land teaches us the importance of being under the voice of spiritual authority and learning to pay reverence to those who are in the seats of leadership over our lives. Don't take those voices for granted. Pray for the spiritual leaders in your life. Even when you can't understand why things are the way they are, open up your ears to what they have to say. When they say, "Things will get better," trust their word because they have walked places that you have never been. When they say, "Things will get better," they will also add words onto that phrase, words that are found in Scripture and remind you that your situation is not the first time someone has been where you have been. The right spiritual voices in your life do not speak from a complacent place where they leave you with a simple pat on the back and some cliché words. No, the right spiritual voices in your life will lovingly point you back to the Truth and remind you that if you keep holding onto faith, all things will be made new.

If you don't have a spiritual mentor in your life, I highly encourage you to pray about it and choose someone who will be able to say the hard things in love and point you in the right direction. Alongside your pastor, who is a voice of authority in your life, mentors can provide accountability and guidance for your life. Their voice of authority in your life might be the very thing that will lead you into the promised land.

God places leaders in our lives not so that we can become mere followers, but so that we can learn to respect their authority to speak against things in our lives that might be hindering us from stepping into the promises that God has for our lives, which may even include your future ministry, family, marriage, fill in the blank.

Before anything else, we have to come into obedience with God's Word as we seek Him in every decision and choice that is made.

When you study the scriptures in Genesis and Exodus, you notice a theme that is brought up over and over again. The promise of inheritance came through obedience unto God.

Are there areas in your life that need to be brought into submission today? Perhaps there is an area of disobedience or lack of discipline that is hindering your entrance into your own promised land. This does not mean to say that every time your promise has not come to pass, you are in disobedience, because oftentimes God uses the delay as a testing ground for our faith. Rather, it simply proposes a question that makes us examines our hearts: Is there anything in my life that is keeping me from crossing my own Jordan River?

This lesson in Joshua teaches us that it is important to check our hearts and align them in obedience to God's Word. Proverbs 6:23 states, "For a command is a lamp, teaching is a light, and corrective discipline is the way to life."

If we are not in the Word of God and connected to a local church, it will be difficult to stay submitted to God and enter the incredible promises that He has for our lives. Your leaders have your best interest at heart, just as Joshua had the best in mind for his people because he was in submission to God.

A spirit of obedience and a spirit of humility will keep you on the path towards God's deliverance into the promised land. And, even if you are still wandering in the desert, wondering when the promise will come to pass, just keep trusting. Keep trusting in the God who put the stars in the sky and knows how many fish are in the sea. That's wild. We can trust our Creator, because He is in control. We are reminded of this in Psalm 8:3-7 when it states, "When I consider Your heavens, the work of Your fingers, The moon and the stars, which You have ordained, what is man that You are mindful of him, And the son of man that You visit him? For You have made him a little lower than the angels, And You have crowned him with glory and honor. You have made him to have dominion over the works of Your hands; You have put all things under his feet."

If there is anything that you may walk away from today, even if you are seeking God for the why to your situation, please know this. God knows what He is doing. Listen to the voices of spiritual authority in your life. And, keep walking in obedience to Him.

4

THE LIGHT WINS

"We are all broken, that's how the light gets in."
-Ernest Hemingway

Growing up, I was lucky enough to spend many happy days at my grandparent's ranch. They live in a small town in Coyote, California on Malech Road. It's true. I'm not making that up. The ranch was established in 1867, which is pretty remarkable to think about, that all these years later, they are still harvesting apricots and sharing them with others. There is nothing better than a Malech Ranch Apricot. Whether it's dried apricots or apricot cobbler, the sweet taste of apricots is summertime to me.

The best part about summertime was getting to spend summers at the ranch with all my cousins, something that my dad and his cousins also spent together. If you talk to anyone in our family, there are plenty of stories to go around for hours. So much mischief, so much fun.

One memory that sticks out to me above the rest is getting together with all my cousins and taking a trip through the underground tunnel. The entrance to the tunnel starts on the ranch side and ends up on the other side of the freeway. For some reason, we never brought flashlights along with us and this was long before any of us had cellphones, so we could not pull out that handy dandy flashlight app for light. So, we did what anyone would do in said situation. We put our hand on the back of the person in front of us and just walked on, hunched over, one by one, clinging to one another, screaming when we came across some rodent, completely surrounded by darkness. It's amazing how when you enter a tunnel, the darkness just engulfs you and it's all you can focus on. You are desperately waiting for the light to flood in. Nearing the end of the tunnel, whenever the light broke through, it was so powerful. Blinding, almost. You take the light for granted when you are always walking in the light. You appreciate the light in a new way after you've been in the darkness for a while.

When we are walking through dark seasons of life, the light of Jesus becomes all the more powerful. It is in the darkness that we search for the light, that we eagerly look for that which we no longer take for granted. In the darkness, we trust that one step later, one day, the light will come bursting through. And, on that day, we will be all the more grateful for the answers that have come at the end of the long and dark tunnel.

On one of the darkest nights that the world has ever known, Jesus became broken so that the light of the Holy Spirit could enter within you and I. When Jesus stood before His accusers before being sent to the cross, He stood in complete silence as the people accused him of charges that he was not guilty of by no means. I know that my human tendency is to immediately argue and make the facts known when someone falsely accuses me. Yet, Jesus stood there in silence when he was falsely accused. That is self-control beyond human will. As the chaos began to die down, they asked Him one more question. Are you the Messiah? It was in this moment that He finally spoke two of the most powerful words ever to be phrased. "I AM."

Jesus became broken for you and I so that He could become our living light, our resurrection power, the Good

Shepherd that guides us through the darkest chapter of our lives and gives us hope when the end of the tunnel seems so far from sight.

Because of what Jesus endured, it is no wonder that we, too, must become broken and face our own dark chapters in order to be made more into God's image. This is why Paul wrote in 1 Peter 4:12-13, "Beloved, do not think it strange concerning the fiery trial which is to try you, as though some strange thing happened to you; but rejoice to the extent that you partake of Christ's sufferings, that when His glory is revealed, you may also be glad with exceeding joy."

In our brokenness, the power of God's redemption is not only able to mend the broken pieces together, but is able to bring glory to His Name when the light overcomes the darkness. The light will win. That's the promise found in Revelation.

Lean in and understand that the Holy Spirit gives you the peace necessary so that even in weak moments, even in the dark chapters of your life, you may find rest in the Father's arms. Through it all, let your light keep shining. The world is looking to the church, to see how Christians will respond in times of difficulty. Matthew 5:13-16 reminds us of who we are, "You are the light of the world. A city that is set on a hill cannot be hidden. Nor do they light a lamp and put it under a basket, but on a lampstand, and it gives light to all who are in the house. Let your light so shine before men, that they may see your good works and glorify your Father in heaven." That last part is so key. *That they may glorify your Father in heaven.*

When it doesn't make sense, don't try to tune into every radio station trying to find an answer. Tune into the Holy Spirit, for by it, when difficulty comes your way, you will respond in a way that won't make sense to others. When you sing with hope in your lungs, your life, on the darkest of days, will bear a bright light that draws others to Christ.

I want to leave you with words that I found in one of my journals from a few years ago. It reads, "Darkness will not win. The cross has defeated sin. And, redemption is forevermore.

Do not lose heart, child. You are not God and you cannot make sense of this world and all that takes place, but put your trust in God. You are truly in the shelter of His wings. Wandering in the dark, may you find the light and press forward. The greatest light, God's Holy Spirit, dwells inside of us. Let His light be your guide on the foggiest of mornings."

Selfless love
He thought of you and I before time ever began
With nailed & bruised hands
With false accusations
With humiliation at the forefront of every step,
The one who created you and I
Stood in silence
Until He made His presence known to all
"I AM"
He revealed himself to mankind
In the darkest of hours
In the same way God revealed Himself to Moses
"I AM"
Pain spilled
A pool of blood at His feet
With every sin of mankind brooding there
He knew when He said
"Let there be light"
That the day would come
When darkness would cast its shadow
And His created image would no longer see His face
Until the promise came to pass
"I AM"
Beginning to end,
Alpha and Omega
Come into His marvelous light
And, see for yourself
The glory of
The Great I AM
For, he walked through the darkness
So, that one day
We could see Him face to face
And, be forevermore
With Him in eternal light

5

HIS TIMING, NOT MINE

"Our willingness to wait reveals the value we place on the
object we are waiting for."
-Charles Stanley

"If it is right, it happens-the main thing is not to hurry.
Nothing good gets away."
-John Steinbeck

Just because God says not yet, it doesn't mean it's a no. His
timing is perfect. Always. Sometimes, we need to stop trying to
make it happen and see that God will make it happen
according to His perfect will. In every season, the most
important lesson is to continually allow the preeminence of
Jesus to guide your every day.

When we try to make things happen our way due to lack of
patience and frustration, we end up pushing back the time in
which God wants to work in our lives. When Sarah could not
get pregnant from Abraham, she offered her husband to her
maid due to her strong desire to want a child in the timing she
saw fit as being the perfect time to have a child.

Yet, God had a better plan. Years later, God came to Sarah
and told her that she was to have a son, which had her

laughing at God. I can only imagine Sarah being in disbelief as she wondered, "Now? You are going to give me a child now? Where were you thirty years ago?"

Have you ever had a moment in your life where you have had a similar attitude as Sarah did? I'll be the first among all of us to say that I know I have. **I wonder if our attitudes and our lack of patience hinders the time in which God wants to come and work in our lives.**

"Jesus replied, 'You don't understand what I'm doing now, but someday you will.'"
John 13:7

It is important to understand that while we do not understand what God is doing, He is the Author of all time, from beginning to end. Our concept of time is so different from God's concept of time. In fact, such a word doesn't even exist in His vocabulary. He is able to see ALL things whereas we can only see the present and past moments that we have lived through.

Think of past circumstances that were difficult while you were going through them, but when you look back, you can see that God's hand was in it all along. You might even tell yourself, "Wow. I wish I had worried less about that." With that mindset, whatever it is that is worrying you today, let go and give that over to God. We know that God always has a plan, and when we surrender our plans over to Him, He will be able to guide us accordingly.

If it is right, it will happen in God's way, the way that knows all things work together for good to those who love the Lord. The fact of the matter is that God is able to work all things, whether good or bad, and bring them together for our good.

And, lastly, don't try to force open a door that was never yours to open to begin with. **The right career, relationship, and opportunity will open at the right time. Remember, nothing good gets away.** So, rather than focusing on the doors that have not yet opened, cherish the room that you are currently sitting in. Set your eyes on the beauty of this day. Don't be so fixated on the future that you miss the season that you are in.

Recently, in a season where I was getting frustrated that nothing was going according to my plan, I became really convicted by the gentleness of God's voice: Don't force something that I've already planned.

Don't force God's will. Don't force open the door, especially if it's a door that God never intended for you to walk through. How do you know that it's the right door? Wait on the LORD. Trust in Him. And, at the right time, He will give you the key. And, it will be 100% worth it.

Lamentations 3:22-26 reminds us, "Through the Lord's mercies we are not consumed, Because His compassions fail not. They are new every morning; Great is Your faithfulness. 'The Lord is my portion,' says my soul, 'Therefore, I hope in Him!' The Lord is good to those who wait for Him, to the soul who seeks Him. It is good that one should hope and wait quietly."

Time moves quickly
Thousands of faces pass on by
And leave inevitable memories
While the watch on my wrist
Chimes tick tock

Time moves forward
And, although the fog is thick
I keep making memories
While my ears tune into
The gentle ticking of the clock

And, although, I cannot see
Through the fog and across the Bay
I know the other side exists
And, I will arrive there
If I will simply let go
And, trust that He truly does know
Only time will tell

6

MOUNTAIN MOVER

"The moment you start to move, the mountain starts to move."
-Olafur Eliasson

"Faith can move mountains."
-Matthew 17:20

A few summers ago, I had the wonderful opportunity to hike the Andes Mountains in the beautiful country of Peru. It was a four-day trek to reach our destination point of Machu Picchu, one of the seven wonders of the world. I have ran two half marathons and multiple other races in my lifetime, and I have to say that those races had absolutely nothing on this trek. The trek to Machu Picchu was the most physically enduring four days of my life, but so worth it in the end. One day, in particular, we hiked over 5,000 ft to get through the pass and onto the other side, which had my muscles begging me to never make them go on a trek again. News flash. I definitely would go on another trek. It's an incredible experience. I haven't consulted my muscles how they feel about that just yet.

During the hike, I realized that if I had not been equipped before going to Peru, there would have been no way that I would have been able to overcome that mountain. And, perhaps I would have been able to, but let me tell you, it would have been that much more of a difficult task. The same is with our spiritual lives. So often we want to overcome the mountains in our lives, but we don't want to go through the training.

When I hiked Machu Picchu, I couldn't afford to chance my life on cheap equipment and training. We can't afford Cheap Christianity or cheap tools to get us to the place that God has in store for us.

Each person's training will be different, but each person will be using the same tools to train for this journey called life. There are tools in a Christian's life that are absolutely necessary. Whether you are just beginning this journey with God or have been walking with Him for fifty years, I want to remind us all how important it is for daily time spent with God. What does this look like? We spend it with Him through prayer and the reading of His Word. If we were to go days without talking to our friends and family, we not only would grow distant from one another, but we would have no way of knowing their heartbeat. This is why daily devotion is absolutely vital.

More so, as we grow in our relationship with God, it is all the more important to become equipped with the right tools for this life. So, here's some hefty reading to get this point across. Ephesians 6:10-18 states, "Finally. My brethren, be strong in the Lord and in the power of His might. Put on the whole armor of God, that you may be able to stand against the wiles of the devil. For we do not wrestle against flesh and blood, but against principalities, against powers, against the rulers of the darkness of this age, against spiritual hosts of wickedness in the heavenly places. Therefore take up the whole armor of God, that you may be able to withstand in the evil day, and having done all, to stand. Stand therefore, having girded your waist with truth, having put on the breastplate of righteousness, and having shod your feet with the preparation of the gospel of peace; above all, taking the shield of faith with which you will be able to quench the fiery darts of the wicked one. And take the helmet of salvation, and the sword of the Spirit, which is the word of God."

It is important that we be prayerful and take up the whole armor of God. We can't do this on our own, but need God's Holy Spirit to guide us with these tools that He entrusts to us. And, just as it requires time to build up stamina to hike a mountain or run a marathon, it is the same with our spiritual walk with God. We aren't going to have this down overnight. Because Jesus is our trek guide, we should be able to trust that He knows the best trails, the times when we need to rest, and the moments when we need to just keep on going.

If you have never read Donald Miller's *A Million Miles in A Thousand Years*, I highly suggest it. He writes this after hiking the same trail that I did in Peru:

"Because you can take a bus to Machu Picchu; you can take a train and then a bus, and you can hike a mile to the Sun Gate. But the people who took the bus didn't experience the city as we experienced the city. The pain made the city more beautiful. The story made us different characters than we would have been if we had skipped the story and showed up at the ending an easier way."

If we didn't have to face mountains in our lives, we would be characters who never developed. The difficult mountains that we face in this life teach us how to truly depend on God. It is in the climb that we grow all the stronger. Because of the mountains we have encountered, we will be better equipped to help others on their own journey. We will know the tools that will be necessary to help them not only survive the mountain, but thrive while they are in the midst of the climb.

Friend, I want you to know this. At the end of the day, when you finally reach the other side, it will be all the sweeter because the lessons you learned along the way have only made you stronger.

As I hiked through the Andes Mountains, God spoke so clearly to me on the third day. The fog was thick all around us as I felt that I truly was living straight out of Ben Stiller's *The Secret Life of Walter Mitty*. As I stood there in the coolness of the evening, surrounded by the wonder of the Andes Mountains, I tightened my scarf around my neck and took a deep breath. As I stood there for a sweet moment, completely mesmerized by creation, God asked me a question, and I think He asks of you the same. **"If I can move mountains, how much more can I do in your life?"**

7

FOR WEARY MORNINGS

"Even the darkest night will end and the sun will rise"
-Victor Hugo

"But those who trust in the Lord will find new strength.
They will soar high on wings like eagles.
They will run and not grow weary.
They will walk and not faint."
Isaiah 40:31

I don't know if it's because I grew up in a home that was always on the go, but for whatever reason, I have a hard time resting. On the weekends, I am typically out of the house before 9AM because sitting by myself for too long drives me crazy. When I travel, sitting by the poolside and doing nothing sounds like purgatory. Okay, that might be a little over dramatic, but there's some truth in it. I know I can't be the only one, but the idea of rest is something that I struggle to grasp. But as much as I'm not a fan of rest, one thing I have really learned is that rest is essential not only for our physical health, but it is necessary for both our mental and spiritual health, too. Also, rest looks differently for everyone. But, whatever rest looks like in your dictionary, it is so important that all of us find the kind of rest that keeps our spiritual vitality in good health. This kind of rest is found in the presence of God, where He is able to give rest to the weary and strength to the faint.

Sometimes, in both ministry and life, we can become really tired. And, rather than taking the time to focus on our body's needs, we can easily throw ourselves into our work. I'm talking to you, America. In a busy, fast paced culture, we become burnt out. If you sometimes feel that you are the only one, you aren't. There are times when we are on top of the moon in ministry and in our personal walk with Christ, but then other times, we are weary and tired to the bone, barely crawling just to stay alive.

There are mornings where it is more difficult than others to get in our daily Bible reading and spend time in prayer. We put forth our human effort, yet feel nothing in return. This is an indication that what we need is more rest. Less time doing, and more time being. It is in the stillness that God's voice speaks to us more clearly. Simply, God wants us to just spend time in His Presence. At a seminar I attended several months ago, a man by the name of Steve Ares told us, "Sometimes, we have to learn how to sit in the silence of heaven." I absolutely love that. Sometimes, God is asking for us to just be still and remember who He is.

Rest is the cessation of motion or action of any kind, and applicable to any being. A body is at rest when it ceases to move. The mind is at rest, when it ceases to be disturbed or agitated.

In the story of John, the closest friends of Jesus had been in mourning and weeping over the death of Jesus Christ, who had now been dead three days. One of those people, Mary, grieved right outside His tomb. The fact that she was near the tomb makes me wonder how much rest she had really gotten over those past few days that Jesus had been dead.

"Now when she had said this, she turned around and saw Jesus standing *there,* and did not know that it was Jesus. Jesus said to her, "Woman, why are you weeping? Whom are you seeking?" She, supposing Him to be the gardener, said to Him, "Sir, if You have carried Him away, tell me where You have laid Him, and I will take Him away." Jesus said to her, "Mary!" She turned and said to Him, "Rabboni!" (which is to say, Teacher)." -John 20:14-16

In this particular scene in John 20, Mary, in her time of mourning and grief, was uneasy and without rest. Now, when Jesus appeared before her, she thought he was a gardener and didn't even recognize him!

Sometimes, we too can become like this. When we are not experiencing the rest we need, we may neglect to recognize Jesus. Rather than taking the time to rest and focus on His Presence, we can easily turn our attention towards the busyness. We become so worried and so focused on the situations that we are walking through that we can't recognize that The Situation is already being taken care of. Jesus is standing right before us saying, "Take heart. I am here. There is no reason to fear. Stay and rest awhile."

We spend a lot of time listening to other voices throughout the day, plugging into media outlets that may appear to be rest for our mind, when in all actuality, true rest can only be found through Christ. If we don't take these moments to find rest in Him, to recover from the strain of everyday life as well as the ministry, we will become spiritually and emotionally burnout.

We can become so busy, even doing the right things with good intentions, that we don't recognize that all along Jesus is right by our side. Place your understanding in the peace of Jesus Christ, a peace that surpasses all understanding.

Colossians 1:20 gives us this promise as we understand that through His reconciliation with mankind, "He made peace with everything in heaven and on earth by means of Christ's blood on the cross."

In a world of everchanging news stories, doctrines, beliefs and values, we can become exhausted. To rest in Christ is to place our confidence in Him, the one who is never changing in every season of life. Rest in Him, weary one.

8

LETTING GO OF MY EXPECTATIONS

"I'm a pencil in the hand of God"
-Mother Theresa

From the moment we are kids, we have expectations for what our lives will look like. From fairy tale stories to the aspirational lives of those we meet or simply admire from a screen, we begin to form our own expectation of what our future should look like. And, that's the danger of the human imagination. Because, though it is such a good thing to dream, and I wouldn't be where I am today without those seeds that were planted in me long ago, the danger is when life doesn't turn out like we had expected it to. Which, I think, for most of us, is quite true to our circumstances.

I had it all planned out. From the moment I was seven years old, I had dreamt that I would end up in the city of San Diego. It was a family favorite of ours and somewhere where we would often vacation. So, when it came time to apply for colleges, I had applied to all the universities in San Diego that I could, and then a few other universities in other cities, just for good measure. When my mother and I flew down to San Diego for a long weekend to tour each of the campuses, I could feel the anticipation rising in my throat. I was giddy and so excited to meet my new home. After a weekend filled with college tours, seafood, and perfect weather, my mother and I sat in the airport waiting to board our flight home. Sitting there, surrounded by a plethora of people, I began to cry. Now, for anyone who knows me, you know that this is totally outside my character. There's a running joke among my friend group that one day, they will capture some of my tears in a glass jar. Trust me, it's not that I don't cry. My poor pillow has captured plenty of tears over the years. It's just not my favorite thing to do, especially in front of other people. However, I do believe that there is great strength in our tears. Even Jesus wept, showing you and I that tears are healthy and necessary so that we may properly grieve and find strength in our times of need. Okay, commercial break over. Back to the story.

So, there I was, a seventeen-year old girl, who had gone into the weekend so hopeful for her future, completely devastated that she was no longer feeling peace about moving to San Diego. I remember, through tears, looking up at my mom and concluded drastically that I had decided that I would now no longer go to college. It didn't matter that I had worked so hard for the past four years to meet the UC (University of California) standards. My expectation for how my life was supposed to turn out had just completely gone down the drain. I was a teenager who was being dramatic in the middle of an airport. If I could go back in time, I would return to that airport and look that girl in the eyes and say, "Relax. This won't be the first time you will have to let go of your expectations. You have a lot to learn, kid."

It turns out that I did not have to let go of my dream of going to university, but I just had to let go of the life that I had planned for myself since I was seven years old. And, to my surprise, I ended up in the place I had told myself I would absolutely never move to: Los Angeles. God has a sense of humor.

During that moment in the airport, I was so fixated on my own plan that I had managed to miss the huge blessing before me. I should have realized that no matter where I ended up, I had the opportunity to go to college, which is such a huge privilege. I don't take one day of my education for granted and thank God every single time I get to pay my college loans. Today, I know this more than anything, and wish I could tell my younger self that the sooner you learn to let go of the expectations that you have for your life, the easier it will be to step into God's will, without fear or reservation. However, I think each of our younger selves had to learn that lesson in some way or another, and even today, as an adult, I still have to be reminded of this lesson.

Eight years later since breaking down in that airport, I can say that there have been many moments since then where I have had to learn to let go and release my expectations into the hands of God. Sometimes, it's just learning to trust God with the everyday and other times, it's been about releasing my expectations into God's hands when it came to much more serious decisions in life, such as relationships, jobs, family life, etc. **The sooner we let go of our own plans, the easier it will be to grasp the life that God has for us.** Not only did I end up going to college in the Greater Los Angeles area, but I have ended up making an entire life for myself here post-graduation. And, who knows where God will take me in the future. All I know is that I'm going to let Him lead me there.

Does this mean that we should give up on every dream or expectation that we hold for the future? Not entirely. But, I do believe that we must surrender daily every expectation, so that we may experience the life God has planned for us. Because expectation is a very strong belief, when it is not met, it brings about a very strong feeling of disappointment. Disappointment is a letdown, a letdown in either ourselves or in other people, a feeling that arises from our plans not going accordingly, where pain visits and re-visits, making us wonder what is it that we are doing wrong. Questions arise.

But, what I have learned as my life has ended up in situations that I never thought I'd be in is that God is still good in it all. Even when we wonder if He hears our prayers when disappointment comes knocking at our door once again, we must remind ourselves of this truth:

"Am I going to let my circumstances determine my view of God or am I going to let God determine how I view my circumstances?" -Lisa Harper

Through it all, our expectations cannot be placed in our own idea of what comes next, but instead, our expectations must be placed in the hope of who God is. Though I do not know what comes next and though my expectations may be different from my reality, I do know that God is walking with me and that truth, even on very difficult days, brings comfort and joy that reminds me in John 4:15, "but whoever drinks the water I give them will never thirst. Indeed, the water I give them will become in them a spring of water welling up to eternal life."

This verse is such a powerful reminder that once we are filled with God's Spirit, we have been filled with new life, a life that places our expectations in the cross. When we place our expectations at the feet of Jesus, we can become fully satisfied in Him. If we truly believe that our lives are not our own, then when our expectations are not met, we can look at it through the lens of God and say, "Okay, God. I'm going to trust You." In the words of Rick Warren, "God is more interested in your character than your comfort. God is more interested in making your life holy than He is in making your life happy."

Even when your expectations aren't met, even when life gets really uncomfortable, remember that God is far more interested in your character. God is interested in you and I becoming disciples who think less of ourselves and become consumed, instead, by God's mission. And, yes, somewhere, along the way, we will find that God's dreams are far greater than anything we could dream up on our own. Because if I had never ended up in Los Angeles, I would have never met the people who changed my life for the better. I would have never ended up at Life Church where my life was made new in Christ. God knew all along what He was doing.

In Acts 17:27-28, it states, "God did this so that they would seek Him and perhaps reach out for Him and find Him, though He is not far from any one of us. For in Him we live and move and have our being."

When we seek Him and find Him, we will discover that by letting go of our own expectations, we will live and move and have our being. God really does write the best stories.

9

INADEQUATE PURSUIT

"His pursuit is greater than your ability to wander."
-Lisa Bevere

"His son said to him, 'Father, I have sinned against both
heaven and you, and I am no longer worthy of being called
your son.' But his father said to the servants, 'Quick! Bring the
finest robe in the house and put it on him. Get a ring for his
finger and sandals for his feet. And kill the calf we have been
fattening. We must celebrate with a feast, for this son of mine
was dead and has now returned to life. He was lost, but now he
is found.' So the party began."

Luke 15:21-24

When I was in high school, my cousins opened for a band
that was touring through California. They gave me a CD of
this band and I immediately fell in love with their music. My
favorite genre of music is folk/indie. I love poetry, as you will
see throughout this book, and perhaps that is why I love folk
music so much. Folk music is poetic to me, and tells stories of
people's life experiences and places they have been.

So, let's fast forward to college. My dad and I were
checking out my new home, Azusa Pacific University. I was
just a young and naïve Freshman who had no idea what the

next four years would bring. At the time, I didn't realize that they would be defining years for me. Wandering around the campus, I noticed a sign that said there would be a concert out on the lawn that Friday evening. I remember jumping up in excitement as I turned to my dad and exclaimed, "Dad, it's my favorite band!" I was so thrilled. Come to find out, most of that band attended Azusa Pacific. Sometimes, our worlds collide in the most wonderful of ways.

All of this to say, there are words from that first album that my cousins first gave me that has stuck with me all these years later. So, here they are. Thank you to the band, Branches.

I came out to the desert
To find what I lost in your eyes
I filled my lungs with the sunset
And walked out into the night
I am a wandering soldier
In this dusty land
Nothing but the torn clothes on my back
And the empty barrel in my hand
"Onwards, broken-hearted soldier
Into the great unknown
Lay down your weapons and follow
Into the light of the sun"

Over the years, I have felt a lot like a wandering soldier, just trying to find my place called home. In the past ten years, I have lived in fifteen different places that I temporarily called home. One summer, while living in the desert of Las Vegas, God shifted my heart to find what I had lost during the years of wandering, during the years of trying to find my own way. It was monsoon season and it was raining. I lifted my hands in that desert and began to sing the words to the very popular Hillsong song at the time, Oceans.

Spirit lead me where my trust is without borders
Let me walk upon the waters

Wherever You would call me
Take me deeper than my feet could ever wander
And my faith will be made stronger
In the presence of my Savior

When I returned back to college that Autumn, I was baptized in the wonderful name of Jesus. September 22, 2013 will forever be the best day of my life, because I had stopped wandering. I had come home to Jesus. I felt so unworthy of His love, but He revealed to me that He loved me more than I could ever imagine.

Have you ever felt inadequate or unworthy of the love of Jesus Christ? In His embrace, you think of all of your shortcomings, your failures, your mishaps, and of all the times you really let Him down. But, Jesus doesn't want you to live a life with these wondering thoughts. He wants you to accept His forgiveness and His love fully, the best gift that we could ever receive here on earth. The reason September 22, 2013 is the best day of my life is because I became a new person that day. Jesus went to the cross so that you and I could experience His resurrection power. It is the most beautiful gift we could ever receive. And, no matter who you are or how long you have been wandering, this gift is for you, too.

The fact of the matter is that the love of Jesus Christ is indeed undeserving, but He gives it to us freely. That is why baptism is not only necessary, but is a covenant sign that we have been bought by the blood of Jesus Christ. We are His forevermore and nothing can separate us from His love. It is up to you and I if we will continue to wander, or if we are willing to receive such a wonderful gift. The gift of salvation is the greatest gift to mankind.

A lot of us may feel as though we must do good works to earn this love, but this is not true. Jesus reminds us through the parable of the prodigal son, as well as many other stories found throughout the Scriptures, that we are not saved or loved by our works. Our works are a response to the love of the Father, for it is by our faith alone that we are able to experience the true love of Jesus Christ.

Whatever you are carrying, whether it appears to be unnoticeable or heavy, lift those weighty thoughts off of yourself, and accept His pursuit in all its fullness.

We are inadequate for such a pursuit, but He is abundant in grace and mercy as He reminds us that by simply entering into His arms, we are complete. You don't need to approach Him with eloquent words or a fancy suit or dress as He will accept you right where you are, no matter where you've been or what you look like, for you are a child of the King. **You can beat yourself up and allow yourself to remain beaten when you mess up or you can choose to rise up in God's grace. The choice is yours.**

"For a righteous man may fall seven times AND rise again."
-Proverbs 24:16

It is only by His grace alone that we are no longer seen as inadequate in His pursuit. It is in a place of feeling inadequate that we recognize just how deep the Father's love is for us. Onwards, soldier. Step into the light of the Son.

PURSUED

You are being pursued
Pursued like the wind
Chasing the leaves
In Fall
Looked upon
As a mother who sees
Her child for the first time

Each and every day
Pursued
Loved
Heard

Child, this lullaby
This love letter
This never-ending song
That can't get out of your head
Is forever yours and mine

Here you stand
Not alone
Not silenced
Not rebuked
Not without one to hold

For, His heartbeat
Intertwined with your own
Whispers
"You love because I first loved you."

And, in that moment
You find
In the pain,
In the unknown
In the misunderstanding

Love.
Love.
Love.
Period.
You are loved.

JENNIFER MALECH

10

IT IS WELL WITH MY SOUL

"The peace and fulfillment of Jesus is literally so good that your bank account can be empty, your body be sick and your heart be broken, but it can always be well with your soul."
-Charles Spurgeon

Horatio Spafford, writer behind the well renowned hymn, *It is well with my soul*, speaks to the very reason for our human existence. When you learn about the origin of the hymn, you come to realize that Spafford had a powerful understanding about life; he did not place his hope in this life, but rather, he placed it in the one to come.

After the Great Chicago fire put Spafford in financial ruin, he would go on to lose his four daughters at sea, his wife the only survivor. Rather than cursing God, and believing that His Creator had turned against him, he wrote a song that we are all very familiar with. It goes like this:

When peace like a river, attendeth my way,
When sorrows like sea billows roll;
Whatever my lot, Thou hast taught me to know

It is well, it is well, with my soul.

Though Satan should buffet, though trials should come,
Let this blest assurance control,
That Christ has regarded my helpless estate,
And hath shed His own blood for my soul.

My sin, oh, the bliss of this glorious thought!
My sin, not in part but the whole,
Is nailed to the cross, and I bear it no more,
Praise the Lord, praise the Lord, O my soul!

For me, be it Christ, be it Christ hence to live:
If Jordan above me shall roll,
No pang shall be mine, for in death as in life,
Thou wilt whisper Thy peace to my soul.

When you know the story behind the song, it makes the words all the more powerful. Have you ever been in a church service and listened to someone worship unreservedly, and knowing their testimony, it just brings you to complete tears? I can only imagine how Spafford's wife responded when he first shared these words with her. Even in seasons of pain and uncertainty, Spafford recognized that we could still experience true joy here on earth.

When you find Jesus and recognize the gift that you have in Him: the gift of salvation, a gift that this world is so hungry and thirsty for, a gift that grants everlasting life, your soul can't help but burst from its seams with supernatural joy.

The peace and fulfillment of Jesus Christ fills our souls with a deep and abiding joy, with great hope for the world to come, and great peace for the promises that He has given you and I. Oh, it is the greatest gift to get to love Him and be known by Him. **When we shift our perspectives from looking at ourselves and look instead towards heaven, we**

will discover life's purpose and greatest joy.

James 1:2-5 states, "My brethren, count it all joy when you fall into various trials, knowing that the testing of your faith produces patience. But let patience have its perfect work, that you may be perfect and complete, lacking nothing. If any of you lacks wisdom, let him ask of God, who gives to all liberally and without reproach, and it will be given to him."

I am certain you have heard this before, but life is an endurance race, not a sprint. When we face various trials, we become better equipped to complete the race marked before us. More so, when the journey was arduous to get to the end, there is greater joy when we finally do reach the finish line. So, wherever you are in your race, remember that in all legs of the journey, God is with you every step of the way. Sometimes, we just have to take it one day at a time.

EVERLASTING JOY

Like stained glass
My tears make a mark
Like prison walls
My hands grasp for an escape

The thickening fog
Has spent chills through my spine
And, deep thunder
Has the crewmen in an uproar

Yet, it is here
Here that I find
In the deep recesses of my soul

Stillness

Through stained tears on a shipyard's deck
An inevitable melody
Comes forth through my throat
As salvation song reminds me

His joy is everlasting
His truth is unfailing
So, I will endure the race
Knowing He never forsakes us

In the midst of the storm
He has taught me to sing
It is well
It is well with my soul

11

WAITING THROUGH UNANSWERED PRAYERS

"Amidst the confusion of the times, the conflicts of conscience, and the turmoil of daily living, an abiding faith becomes an anchor to our lives."
-Thomas S.Monson

In his book Mere Christianity (which I highly recommend by the way), C.S. Lewis writes, "I do not know why there is this difference, but I am sure that God keeps no one waiting unless He sees that it is good for him to wait. When you do enter your room, you will find that the long wait has done you some kind of good which you would not have had otherwise. But you must regard it as waiting, not as camping. You must keep on praying for light: and of course, even in the hall, you must begin trying to obey the rules which are common to the whole house. And above all you must be asking which door is the true one; not which pleases you best by its paint and paneling."

wait. (v). stay where one is or delay action until a particular time or until something else happens

It is one of the least fun/unlikable responses that we could ever receive from anyone. Especially for Americans who live in a very fast-paced society, waiting does not come naturally. As humans, we want answers now. And, furthermore, we want to be in control of what is to come next. So, when we are told to just wait, our initial response is to try to figure things out on our own. But, God reminds you and I that we must wait on Him. The waiting requires a strength that is beyond our own natural will. Through the power of the Holy Spirit, we are given the strength to wait through unanswered prayers. While God's plans and His ways are a mystery, to which at times His plans don't even make sense, we must learn to sometimes become comfortable with no answer.

A couple autumns ago, on my red eye flight to Iceland, I had only been en route for less than an hour when the pilot announced that we were to take an emergency landing in Las Vegas. There was a medical emergency with one of the travelers which resulted in a three-hour delay on ground in which we weren't even allowed to leave the airplane. It was stuffy and hot. It was two in the morning. We had a lot of questions, but the stewardesses were giving us no answers. ***Waiting is a very uncomfortable state to be in.***

As I sat there on the runaway in Las Vegas, I sunk back into my seat as I realized that I would miss my connecting flight in Reykjavik. I was supposed to have a short layover in Iceland and then hop over on a connecting flight to London that day. After the realization that I would be missing my connecting flight, I frantically called my dad and asked if he could see if there were any other flights leaving for London from Iceland that day. Nope. There were none. At this point, as we sat on the runaway waiting, I thought about how I was not looking forward to staying a night in Iceland alone. My friend, Samantha, was already in London, and I began to wonder if she would have to enjoy our England vacation all on her own.

Why is it that our minds quickly jump to the worst possibility when we are in a time of waiting?

Even though the pilot ensured us that we would be back in the air soon, I had very little hope that we were to ever leave Las Vegas before sunrise. Yet, what I quickly learned, (because yes, I did make it to Iceland and then to London. They held all the connecting flights in Reykjavik for the day. There are some perks when you have a connecting flight at a very small International airport), was that all of my worrying, fretting and frantic planning for something that would never even take place had been futile. The stewardess and the pilot had assured us that it would all work out because what did they have that I didn't have? They had more knowledge about the overall ways in which their airport and trafficking patterns work.

The reality is that we are passengers in this life who have to learn how to trust the pilot of our lives. We have to believe that God is working even when we are just sitting on the runaway, going absolutely nowhere, because God has knowledge that we don't have access to.

Oswald Chambers writes, "All that is required is to live a natural life of absolute dependence on Jesus Christ. Never try to live your life with God in any other way than His way. And His way means absolute devotion to Him. Showing no concern for the uncertainties that lie ahead is the secret of walking with Jesus."

In absolute devotion to Jesus, we find what it means to be truly surrendered to Christ-to show no concern for the uncertainties that lie ahead. If we truly believe that God is working all things together for good, then when our prayers go unanswered, when life goes on and everyone else seems to be getting an answer, yet we are still left with very little clarity on our circumstances, we will still be able to trust God, knowing that in the waiting, we(if we learn to be still and rest in the knowledge of God) are becoming more like Christ.

Every once in a blue moon, I read from The Message version of the Bible, and I love the translation for this familiar passage of scripture. Romans 8:26-28 states, "Meanwhile, the moment we get tired in the waiting, God's Spirit is right alongside helping us along. If we don't know how or what to pray, it doesn't matter. He does our praying in and for us, making prayer out of our wordless sighs, our aching groans. He knows us far better than we know ourselves, knows our pregnant condition, and keeps us present before God. That's why we can be so sure that every detail in our lives of love for God is worked into something good."

As we wait through unanswered prayers, be reassured that when you completely devote yourself to Jesus Christ, even when it feels like you have received no answer, you have. In the same way that Job came to this revelation in Job 42:3, "Therefore I have uttered what I did not understand. Things too wonderful for me, which I did not know," we too must recognize the authority of God's plan, to which we are finite in understanding. In fact, even if God tried to reveal it to us, I believe it would still be far beyond our understanding. We aren't here on earth to have our own will accomplished, but to have God's will accomplished through His earth, and we are that earth. Waiting on God forces us to recognize that our purpose as children of the King is so that His glory may be revealed throughout all the earth. Our unanswered prayers will fulfill His greater purpose.

12

THE ROAD LESS TRAVELED

"Two roads diverged in a wood, and I-I took the one less traveled by, And that has made all the difference."
-Robert Frost

Choosing the Christian life is to choose the road less traveled. When you first venture out on this road with Christ, it can be easy to want to turn back around and be pulled towards the more popular route.

It is important for us to learn that just because we live with Christ, does not mean that we will be exempt from trials and tribulations. In fact, it pretty much is a guarantee that there will most certainly be difficulties, for it is in some of the most difficult seasons of life that an individual becomes more like Christ.

Paul wrote in 1 Peter 4:12-14, "Beloved, do not think it strange concerning the fiery trial which is to try you, as though some strange thing happened to you; but rejoice to the extent that you partake of Christ's sufferings, that when His glory is revealed, you may also be glad with exceeding joy. If you are reproached for the name of Christ, blessed *are you,* for the Spirit of glory and of God rests upon you. On their part He is blasphemed, but on your part He is glorified."

As Christians, we can rejoice in times of suffering because we know that our lives are meant to glorify Christ. And, whether it's in this life or the next, His Glory will be revealed. As we surrender ourselves over to Christ and lay everything at His feet, He will give us the strength necessary to fight and win the race. Through the sanctification process, a pruning process that rids of the thorns in our own lives that cannot belong, my "self" becomes fully identified in Christ.

The road less traveled is a life of sacrifice. Paul also shares with us in 1 Corinthians 15:31 that "I affirm, by the boasting in you which I have in Christ Jesus our Lord, I die daily." We must die daily. This isn't a physical death, of course, for that would be quite alarming, but rather it is a death to our flesh's will. Paul had to learn, just as we have to learn, who all of this is for. We have to submit our daily hopes and dreams to Christ, because ultimately, we want His glory to be revealed. This is a common theme found throughout this book, but it's because I want you and I to grasp that when life gets really muddy, we can still have hope for what is ahead, because this life doesn't belong to us to begin with. And, let me tell you, living for God is the best decision I ever made. My friend Sarah once told our small group, **"I would rather go through my worst day with God than go through my best day without Him."** So very true!

The problem with man today, and with man since the beginning of humanity's timeline, is that while we desire God, we also want to keep our self. There are many of us, myself included, who have been naturally drawn to pursue the pride of life, the more traveled road here on earth. 1 John 2:16 states, "For all that *is* in the world—the lust of the flesh, the lust of the eyes, and the pride of life—is not of the Father but is of the world." If we are to truly live for God, we must surrender ALL that we are to Him. Our full identity is in Christ alone and when we identify fully with Him, it becomes easier to surrender every aspect of our life over to Him, including our careers, our relationships, and our own dreams and desires for the future.

The choice is yours and mine. Do we take the road less traveled by taking on the name of Christ? Or, are we too absorbed in our "self" and what everyone else thinks is best for us that we deny ourselves the most incredible journey?

There have been so many times that I have sought my will above His own because I struggled to give my ALL to Him. There have been times that I tried to do things my own way, and what I quickly realized was this: is if I continue to have one foot in the waters of self and one foot in the waters of God, I would be tossed between two currents that would never allow me to move in one direction. If we are not completely sold out to His Truth and His will, then when resistance comes in the waters of life, we will lose our foundation from which we must be anchored by. When God revealed to me that I was trying to do things my own way, even down to my writing, I became humbled realizing that it is not by self that the Kingdom moves forward, but by His power alone. In asking for God's forgiveness, I prayed that my life would be done His way. We must be people after God's own heart and in order to do so, we must seek His will above our own.

Social media is a wonderful thing, but if we become so focused on our image that we neglect to reflect His image off the screen, then we must have a heart check. Are we so focused on trying to build our kingdom or His Kingdom? What are our motives? If it is anything apart from being motivated by Jesus, then we must repent before God. We all struggle with different things, whether that be greed, the pride of life, jealousy, etc. If we aren't careful, social media can be the perfect space to feed those unwanted emotions. Even in our prayers, it can be so easy to get consumed by the self that we neglect to seek God's heart. My prayer is that we would push aside our self and truly seek God's heartbeat in a new way like never before.

God wants to take you and I to new places that we have never been before, but in order to do that, we first have to go through a process of sanctification that allows God to remove the things that do not belong in His temple, and we are that temple. Through the process of sanctification, you will come to realize that there are places that you will no longer be able to go to, things you won't be able to consume or watch, music you won't be drawn to listen to, environments you won't be allowed to engage in, because God is calling you to something higher. Your body is sacred and meant to be set apart to bring glory and honor to the Kingdom. Those who are without His Spirit will be drawn to the holiness that resides within you, which is why we must pursue sanctification, to be made in the like image of Christ. Because, without knowing it, others will be drawn to Christ due to our steadfast faithfulness to pursue a life of holiness. In today's world, the body is being misused and glorified in an unholy way. Just take a look at Hollywood. I live in Los Angeles, so trust me, I am perfectly aware of Hollywood's agenda. My only word of advice is not to look to Hollywood for guidance on how you should live your life. There is no self-guide book or magazine that will lead you to the answers you are searching for. There is no beauty tip, workout routine, finance class, leadership book that will lead you to fulfillment. It might feed a piece of yourself, but it will not fulfill you in the way that only Christ alone can do.

The enemy will do whatever he can to get our minds fixated off Christ and onto our self. It is why, when you are going through difficult times, the enemy will plant fear, doubt, and whatever else, for you to lose focus off God. Please, hear these words. And, don't just brush through them. **The enemy's agenda is to get our minds set on our self, which is empty and inadequate without God. God's agenda is for us to get our minds fixated on Him, through which we find our true self.** God is drawing this generation to sanctification, especially in a day and age where the land is rampant with sin. It means that we will have to take the less popular road, but it will be worth it. Our life is but a mere vapor, a VERY short period in time in comparison to the eternal glory that we will receive at the end of the road less traveled.

13

SAYING GOODBYE TO THE COMFORT ZONE

"To step toward your destiny, you will need to step away from your security."
-*Craig Groeschel*

As humans, we do not like change. We prefer comfort and security as it is a natural tendency for us all. We prefer knowing what's going to happen in the next hour, the next day, the next week, and the next month. We want our human input on how everything should happen accordingly. Have you ever planned out a date night, a vacation, or a self-day to reboot and nothing, absolutely nothing went according to plan?

I learned awhile ago that no matter how many times I make plans, they never seem to go accordingly. And, the more that I try to plan my life out, God seems to always make better plans. This is why I don't have a five year or ten-year plan for my life. I may have goals and aspirations for the next several years, which we should all have, but I don't have set in stone plans. The more I become committed to my plans, the more I will hold onto them for my dear life, not realizing that I am robbing myself of God's most precious gift.

Sometimes, we hold onto things for so long, not surrendering to God's particular plan. Meanwhile, God is reminding us that He has something better in store for us. He knows us better than we know ourselves.

A surrendered heart learns that we have to step outside of our comfort zones and outside that of which is familiar in order for God to do His work in us. We have to be willing to allow God to change our plans so that He may be able to open new doors and allow us to embark on new adventures. While these steps may be outside our comfort zone and daily planner, from time to time, these moments are absolutely necessary for what God wants to do in your life.

No one grows living in the comfortable, no one experiences new things if they always cling to the familiar and become satisfied with where they are. The sooner we learn to embrace the changing tidal waves of life and step outside our comfort zones, God will expand our plans.

A friend recently told me, "Sometimes what we want is not what we need." I echo her words and believe that **the sooner we let go of that which is familiar, the easier it will be to grasp the life that God has for us.** What I'm learning now, more than ever, is that letting go has given me the freedom to live in the uncertain and the uncomfortable with a certainty that God is in control.

Last year, I had the wonderful opportunity to travel to Morocco with my SoCal family. Side note: The church is so awesome. In my immediate family, the nearest relative is hundreds of miles away, so I am so grateful for the families that have adopted me here in SoCal. That's the beauty of the church. No matter your family situation, through the church, you have a family. It's a wonderful thing.

Okay, back to Morocco. Steph, Nick, Zach and I arrived in the dusty streets of Marrakech. The city honestly looks like the renditions of the Streets of Bethlehem program they used to put on in my city every Christmas. It is an entirely different world. When we stepped out into the city, I was uncomfortable to say the least. When we were outside the four walls of our hotel, it was pure madness with crowded streets, smells of the most interesting kinds, and aggressive street vendors (we literally got yelled at when we didn't buy something from someone's store. It's not every day that you get called a fake American). But, once we entered the oasis of where we were staying, there was such peace, as though the outside world didn't exist. That's what God does. In the chaos, you can find peace. When your outside world is uncomfortable, you can breathe and know that God is still in control. But, we didn't remain in the oasis. Because, we weren't intended to just remain in the oasis. We had to step outside our comfort zone. So, we returned to the city streets, enjoyed fresh squeezed orange juice and met new people that shaped our perspective into something new and beautiful. **Sometimes, it takes stepping outside your comfort zone for you to learn things about life and God that you wouldn't any other way.** It is being in cities and situations that make us uncomfortable that prompts us to put our ultimate trust in God.

Don't be afraid to step away from the comfortable. Peter had to step away from his security as a fisherman in order to follow Jesus towards his calling as a disciple of Jesus Christ. Ultimately, it led Peter to be a witness and carrier of the gospel.

In Matthew 16:18-19, the Word of God states,
"And I tell you that you are Peter, and on this rock I will build my church, and the gates of Hades will not overcome it. I will give you the keys of the kingdom of heaven; whatever you bind on earth will be bound in heaven, and whatever you loose on earth will be loosed in heaven."

This would never have been possible if Peter had decided to live inside his comfort zone. Perhaps there are areas in your life that God is prompting you to step towards, whether that be to teach someone a bible study, to write a song and minister through music, to step into a new ministry, to purchase a plane ticket to go on a Missions trip, or to move to a region where God wants you to plant a church or whatever else it may be. The things that God wants to do through His people is endless. We just have to be willing to leave our own security and understand that God is our ultimate security.

It has been so amazing to see the faithfulness of God when His people step outside their comfort zones. In my own personal life, I have seen the power of God work in extraordinary ways when I finally learned to let go and trust God. Was it easy? No. But, every single time, God has shown up in ways that I could have never predicted. **It is His power working in us that leads to transformation around us.** My pastor always tells our church that if you want to grow in your own relationship with God, teach a bible study. When you reach out to those who aren't connected to the church or those within the church who are so hungry to grow in their own personal walk with God, you will get ahold of God's heartbeat and will never be the same again. There is nothing more fulfilling than teaching someone a bible study. There is a time for us to learn and grow, and then there is a time for us to pour back into the lives of those around us.

God calls us into different ministries, and at times it will be uncomfortable, but it is so worth it. I believe that the sooner we learn that this life isn't about us, the easier it will become to leave the unfamiliar and step out in faith into the unknown. I talk about this later on, but I believe that fear is one of the emotions that hinders us from becoming what God has called us to be. The enemy has tried to use fear to trap us from carrying out the Great Commission. But, when you remember who you are and that you belong to the King, you can step out onto the battlefield and know that God is fighting for you, just like David did when he faced Goliath and won.

There are keys to the Kingdom that God wants to give you, but He can't give them over to you if you cling to the comfortable. The uncomfortable reminds us that we must continually put our ultimate trust in Jesus. When we are led by His Spirit and lean on His strength alone, I promise you that He will show up. And, once again, He will amaze us.

14

THE BLESSEDNESS OF POSSESSING NOTHING

"The way to deeper knowledge of God is through the lonely valleys of soul poverty."
-Thomas S. Monson

I fear that in the 21st century church we put too much of a price tag on things, experiences and people to fulfill a certain hunger within, a hunger that takes place when the preeminence of Jesus Christ is no longer our greatest concern.

Why are there so many songs, books, movies and television shows about love or the idea of love? I believe we create out of a deep longing for that which we were created for: a love that requires giving up everything, yet then attaining everything in the process.

Tozer writes, "There is within the human heart a tough fibrous root of fallen life whose nature is to possess, always to possess...things have become necessary to us, a development never originally intended."

As long as we keep chasing our own desires, we will never become fully satisfied in Christ. It is through true satisfaction in Christ alone that we will find life's greatest fulfillment. I know it's such a simple truth, but finding God, truly becoming satisfied in Him alone, will bring us the joy and fulfillment that we are so thirsty for.

"Though you have not seen him, you love him; and even though you do not see him now, you believe in him and are filled with an inexpressible and glorious joy, for you are receiving the end result of your faith, the salvation of your souls." 1 Peter 1:8-9

There are moments in our lives when we experience trials and tribulations of various kind, but it is in these moments, we come to find God and depend on Him in a way that we hadn't when we were living in abundance.

There is a blessedness in possessing nothing, whether that be lack of emotional or physical possession. For in the lonely valleys of soul poverty, your soul will come to truly understand and find that Jesus is your everything.

As mentioned throughout this devotional, I live in the Greater Los Angeles Area. After graduating from college, I moved into my own apartment. As an extrovert, this is somewhat of a nightmare, especially since Los Angeles traffic keeps me from seeing any of my friends or church family during the week. In the past few years since moving out on my own, loneliness has come in waves, like the high tide that unexpectedly comes in and gets your beach set-up all wet, an area that you thought was perfectly safe and dry just moments ago.

When I first moved out on my own, not only did I experience loneliness, but my entry level job post-graduation meant that I was going to have to trust God in a new way with my finances. Because if He didn't come through, then I wouldn't have a roof over my head. I began to depend on God as a child depending on her Father to take care of her everyday needs. Oatmeal became my lifeline during that season. Shout out to my spiritual mama, Steph, who showed up to church with boxes of oatmeal every Sunday. Needless to say, I learned to appreciate things that I used to take for granted in a whole new way, like food on my table and having enough money for the bills to be paid.

It was in this season, though, that God taught me one of the most valuable lessons of all. While loneliness came in waves, it never stayed. It returned back to where it came from when I fixated my eyes off of the situation and focused, instead, on the goodness of God. **Elizabeth Elliot once said, "Loneliness is a required course for leadership."** When I first read this quote, I took a deep breath and took in every one of those words. In my heart, I realized that loneliness had been such a gift. It took me living on my own for me to trust and depend on God in a new way. During seasons of loneliness, I came to discover that nothing else in my life mattered, but His love. Rather than becoming consumed by the loneliness or emotions of that season, I realized how important it was to allow God to shift my perspective so that I could develop as both a Christian and leader.

Whether it is lack of physical or emotional possession, there is a blessedness in possessing nothing, for in it, we find our everything.

You may not experience physical loneliness, but you may go through periods of emotional loneliness. I have experienced this many a time, too. God may even remove some people and voices from your life so that you may tap into the ministry and giftings that God has for you. When you do experience this, remember who all of this is for. Isaiah 61: 1-3 states, "The Spirit of the Lord God is upon Me, Because the Lord has anointed me to preach good tidings to the poor; He has sent me to heal the brokenhearted, to proclaim liberty to the captives, and the opening of the prison to those who are bound; to proclaim the acceptable year of the Lord, and the day of vengeance of our God; to comfort all who mourn, to console those who mourn in Zion, to give them beauty for ashes, the oil of joy for mourning, the garment of praise for the spirit of heaviness; that they may be called trees of righteousness, the planning of the Lord, that He may be glorified."

As much as there were times when I wished I didn't have to experience loneliness, I also knew that part of it was necessary for the places that God was preparing for me to go. I have woken up with a new gratitude in my heart that is completely overwhelmed by the fact that I know Jesus and that He cares enough about us to take us through the process so that we may be made righteous in His image.

If you are restless and feeling empty today, your Creator is creating something beautiful today. Today is an invitation to step into the fullness of His love. He is enough. Let's stop searching for fulfillment in other places. I promise you that when you seek Him with all that you are, your heart will beat in a new way. And, you won't be able to stop yourself from wanting to share this love with others, because you've discovered that it is the only answer, for Jesus replies in John 14:6 with no truer words, "I am the way, the truth and the life."

Breathe
We did not deserve
Yet, even then
Our culture
Believes in our I
Before the preeminence
of the I AM
And, that is the danger
Of the 21st century
and, the many before
We think we need more
To bring us joy
When His
Breath
That brought us to life
Is saying
I AM enough

15

BE STILL AND KNOW

"God's voice is still and quiet and easily buried under an
avalanche of clamour."
-Charles Stanley

Sometimes, we pray for one thing, yet God answers
differently. Although, the doors that God opens may be
different from that which we prayed or hoped for, we will
come to realize that it was the very thing that we needed.

While we are finite, God is infinite in wisdom and
understanding. As God begins to open up doors that might be
different from our own hopes and dreams, He is asking us if
we are willing to adjust our sails and truly follow His will above
our own.

If you've ever been on a sailboat or boat of any kind, you
will find that the winds are violently loud, which makes it
difficult to hold a conversation with those who are aboard the
deck. In our world, we have many different voices that flood
our minds. From social media, various multi-media platforms,
and even differing opinions from our friends and family, we
are plugged into the noise that surrounds us 24/7. Through

the noise and differing distractions, God beckons us to stillness, a stillness that can only be found when we take the time to spend time with Him alone.

And he said, Go forth, and stand upon the mount before the Lord. And, behold, the Lord passed by, and a great and strong wind rent the mountains, and brake in pieces the rocks before the Lord; but the Lord was not in the wind: and after the wind an earthquake; but the Lord was not in the earthquake. And after the earthquake a fire; but the Lord was not in the fire: and after the fire a still small voice.

1 Kings 19:11-13

As the storms of life surrounded Elijah, he heard God's still small voice because he had learned to wait on the LORD. He did not find God's voice in the earthquakes and fires that equate to the daily noise we are surrounded by. Instead, he found God's voice in the stillness, which happened when he decided to be still. God could have spoken to Elijah through the mighty power of the winds, but He didn't. God spoke to Elijah with a still, small voice.

A few years ago, after I graduated from college, I had to make a big decision. At the time, I was interning in the beautiful state of Washington. Since my family is scattered across the U.S. I didn't have the choice, like others, to go home until I figured things out after college. Nope, instead, I had three weeks until my internship was coming to an end and then, I'd be living off the scraps of my last intern paycheck. I had the choice to stay in Washington with a potential job in the works or I could return to Los Angeles where I had just been offered a job. My immediate response was to reach out to family and friends and ask for their opinions, but what I quickly found was that everyone had something different to say. It honestly left me more confused than anything. While I was on the phone with a good friend, she said, "Okay, I'm going to hang up now. You need to go be with God." I remember that moment so clearly. It was a beautiful summer's day in Poulsbo, Washington. I was hanging out down by the waterfront with the breeze in my face and a decision that had to be made in less than 24 hours. I was terrified that I would make the wrong choice and lead my sailboat to sail in the wrong direction. As I wrestled with which door to walk through, there was a stillness in the air that made me turn to the Word of God. I read God's Word and felt so much peace in that moment. It made me realize that if I would just be still and learn to place my trust in Him, then He would give me the direction I need. I had to let go of the idea that I was about to make the wrong choice and choose, instead, to just be still and trust in Him.

I had to give up my own idea of what I thought my life was going to look like after I graduated from college and adjust my sails according to the winds that God was directing my life by. Just like I mentioned earlier in this book, letting go of our expectations gives us the freedom to walk into our God given destiny.

Friend, it is so important to **remove yourself from the noise of the world and find a place to be alone with God. It is there, in the stillness, that His small, yet mighty voice will be found.**

Whatever life looks like today, whether golden sunshine or stormy clouds, whatever questions you are facing today, be still. Be still and take deep breaths. Be still and know that God is still good. Be still and stand on God's promises, founded in His Word, even when it's taking every fiber of your being to believe. Be still and know that God is fighting for you, that God will not lead you astray, and that God is with you, even when the unexpected happens. Be still and know that resilience is becoming part of your character. Be still and know that this is not the end, but rather the beginning of something we cannot yet see. Courage, dear heart. Those were C.S. Lewis's words and I share them with you. With whatever decisions you are facing today, know that God will give you the courage to face whatever it is and better yet, as long as you are walking with Him, He will always lead your sailboat in the right direction. You only need to be still.

GOD'S STILL VOICE.

In the chaos of the morning, we often forget
To stop and smell the roses
Our two feet scurry with the
ever changing winds
As our hamster wheel minds
Go from one hour to the next

What would it look like
If we stopped to smile
And greet one another with the slightest hello

Where has our world gone?
Where we once had ears to hear
The morning bird's song

We move with the ocean's waves
To and from without even a thought
Where seconds become days
And, days turn into months

How my soul longs for conversation
A place that would listen
As our lips slowly come to speak
Where a stranger is a foreign
quite unfamiliar term

Where has our world gone?

Yet, we cannot change these times
By just turning on a switch

But, what I do know is quite certain
That if I stop to smell the roses
In the chaos of the morning
God's still voice will be found.

JENNIFER MALECH

16

ADJUST YOUR SAILS

"She stood in the storm and when the wind did not blow her
way, she adjusted her sails."
-Elizabeth Edwards

Knowing God, rather than mere knowledge of God, is what
leads to a life of sure faith in times of steadfast uncertainty.
Through daily relationship, we come to know God and His
heartbeat. And, the more we come to know God, the more our
hearts will become aligned with His. That is where the true
change in our lives happens. The kind of change that leads us
to do things we never imagined and chase God given dreams
that will impact our world, one step at a time.

When I graduated from college and moved back to Los
Angeles after spending the summer in Seattle, I moved into my
own apartment. It's been over three years since that day, and as
difficult as it has been at times, it has also been a wonderful
time in my life. There have been so many times that I wished I
had roommates and have tried to persuade many a friend to
move to Los Angeles. (I'm a true extrovert to the core). But,
there is something that has been so beautiful about this time
on my own. It has given me the time to focus on my
relationship with God in such a deep way. Trust me. When you

are used to coming home to an empty apartment, you need a companion. God has been my best friend through it all, someone I can call on when the rustling leaves outside make me think someone is about to barge into my home(ha!) or someone I can lean on when my heart has been heavy with situations that were happening in my life that were outside my own control. Friend, if you are single and living on your own and wish this season would just come to an end, I get it, I really do. But, at the same time, I also know how incredible this season of your life is and it's a time that you will never be able to reverse once you cross over to the other side. No matter where you are at in your life right now, single or married, living with ten thousand roommates or none, walk daily in the Word of God. Read it. Memorize it. Take it in like daily vitamins. Or, if you forget to take your vitamins like I often do, then consume the words as easily as getting sucked in by your favorite television series. The more you read the Word and the more time you spend with God, your life will inevitably change for the good. Your sails will adjust according to the Word of God. You will say goodbye to unhealthy habits, and sometimes, you might even say goodbye to some relationships along the way. It is all necessary and part of the growth process.

The more we become rooted in the Word of God, the more our hearts will be anchored to His Truth which will keep us on the right path towards righteousness. It is in our daily relationship with God that not only do we change, but that our hearts will then beat with our Father's heart, where we adjust our schedules and plans to find ways to serve and love those around us. Our faith isn't something that is meant for just ourselves, but it is meant to be spread to others. So, wherever you are, whatever gifts God has given you, let's spread His love through our words, and our hands and feet. **The secret to a prosperous life is a giving life, the center of God's heartbeat.**

When we hear the word of God, we are built in faith, which again reminds us the importance of making sure we are connected to the local church for "faith *comes* by hearing, and hearing by the word of God." -Romans 10:17

While our walk with Jesus Christ is individual, it is not meant to be done alone. As much as our faith is an anchor for our lives, being in connection with other believers will become the paddles that will continually help steer you in the right direction.

The fact of the matter is that the love of mammon puts God second every time. We must allow God to examine our hearts and remove whatever is hindering us from His love. Amidst the turmoil of daily living, which often includes our finances, our busy schedules, and our mass uncertainties, the only way that we will be able to move forward is if we learn to entrust Him with our resources, a trust that can only be attained through a faith that is built not on the words of others, but on the Word of God.

Faith is learning to give to the Kingdom of God when you have nothing. It is learning to accept God's will and His plan in both times of doors being opened and doors being shut. While our situations change and uncertainty may continually knock at our door, the Word of God will always remain steadfast for it is never changing. The Word of God, in and of itself, is what we must anchor our daily lives by.

When we read the Word of God, we are encouraged by the stories in the Scriptures that reminds us that we are not alone. Whatever you are going through, it is not the first time someone has gone through such situation. Just as the disciples had to learn through times of uncertainty to place their trust in the living Word of God, Jesus Christ, we must do the same.

This steadfast anchor reminds you and I that no matter what we are facing in this life, we can put our trust in the hope of His Word.

JENNIFER MALECH

17

COURAGEOUS HEART

"Courage is resistance to fear, mastery of fear-not the absence of fear."
-Mark Twain

One of my favorite verses of Scripture is Joshua 1:9. It reads, "Have I not commanded you? Be strong and courageous. Do not be afraid. Do not be discouraged, for the Lord your God is with you wherever you go." During the past year, it's been a go-to verse, and one that I have shared with my brother who serves in the U.S. Army. I admire and respect our military so much. It is incredible that there are those who choose a life of sacrifice so that you and I can live and enjoy the freedom that we do. It's a courageous field. As I once again read over this familiar piece of scripture, I began to ask myself: What is courage? What does courage look like in our lives?

Being courageous doesn't mean that you are fearless. Rather, being courageous is stepping out in faith, despite the fear(s) that accompany the very act.

As soldiers who serve in the Army of the Lord, we too must make sacrifices so that one day, if not today, others can experience true freedom in Christ. During your journey as a Christian, there will be different places (deployments so to speak) that God will call you to. Sometimes, it will require even greater sacrifice than you ever anticipated, but remembering who your Commander is will help you to step out in faith.

While the book of Joshua pays its greatest attention to Israel's new leader, Joshua, I want to focus on a different character. A woman by the name of Rahab.

In this particular story, the King of Jericho told Rahab that there were Israelite spies who had been sent out by Joshua to spy the land. The King sent her a message that she must bring out the men who had come to spy on the land. But, rather than exposing the two Israelite spies, she hides them from their enemy and keeps them safe. Before the spies lie down for the night, Rahab speaks to them and says:

> *"I know that the LORD has given this land to you and that a great fear of you has fallen on us...When we heard of it, our hearts melted and everyone's courage failed because of you, for the LORD your God is God in heaven above and on the earth below."*
> *-Joshua 2:10,11*

The people are melting in fear, and despite her own fears, she chooses to listen to her heart and perform an action of true kindness and bravery. Rahab puts her own life at risk for the sake of the people of God, despite any fear or doubt or uncertainty that still lingered in the deep recess of her soul.

Courage, birthed out of faith, dissipates the fears within as the faithful God of the universe reminds us that He has a plan from beginning to end. Due to Rahab's courage, the Israelites were able to seize the city of Jericho and cross the Jordan River and step into the land that they had been promised. And, the beauty of the story is that Rahab, a prostitute, is not only shown kindness but is taken into the new land after a true conversion experience. As though this doesn't show the power of redemption enough, we are reminded that Rahab was in the lineage of King David and Jesus Christ. Wow!

Rahab took a risk. She possessed a certain kind of courage that would carry her into the greatest of all promises. She grew to fear God and develop great reverence for her new leader, Joshua.

What risks is God calling you into today?

In being Christians who are fully equipped with the full armor of God, we must pray for courage, the kind of courage that exhibits our faith to both the believer and the unbeliever. As a child who is fighting in the army of God, you can guarantee that your Commander in Chief will never let you lose the ultimate battle. Sometimes it may require a few losses, a few no's here and there, a few disappointments, a few failures, but if you carry on with courage, despite any lingering fears, you can be guaranteed entry into the land of promise that God has placed upon your life.

JENNIFER MALECH

18

THE POWER OF A THOUGHT

"I am building a house where the floor is made up of strength,
where the walls are crafted of ambition, where the roof is a
masterpiece of forgiveness, I am building myself."
-Noor Unnabar

Thoughts. Thousands of them scroll through our mind just
as sudden as aimlessly scrolling through our social media
accounts. We can't even begin to measure how many invade
our mind every day; however, what we can determine is
whether or not those thoughts will become life giving or not.
We have the choice as to whether we will entertain those
thoughts or surrender them over to God.

The dictionary defines a thought as:
(n) an idea or opinion produced by thinking or occurring
suddenly in the mind

Since the mind is so powerful and has the ability to affect
our emotions, our daily encounters with others, as well as God,
we must be aware of the thoughts that accommodate our daily
walk. **An uninvited thought, if entertained, will lead to loss
every time.**

And, while the mind is powerful, you and I have been given the job, through the power of the Holy Spirit, to take into captivity the very thoughts that will lead to destruction if left unattended.

"We demolish arguments and every pretension that sets itself up against the knowledge of God, and we take captive every thought to make it obedient to Christ." -2 Corinthians 10:5

It is important to note that there are no pre-qualifications, nor any degree that you have to earn to serve in the Kingdom of God. There is no background that is better than another, for at the end of the day, we are all children of God. No matter who you are, God want to use your life to make His name known. All that God requires is a life of obedience.

As we discover what God's will for our lives looks like, there are many different emotions that we face. Of these emotions, one of the most dangerous is fear. It is fear that hinders us from life's greatest opportunities. Simply put, fear paralyzes us. However, I believe that fear is an emotion that we can conquer through the help of the Holy Spirit.

fear.

(n). an unpleasant emotion caused by the belief that someone or something is dangerous, likely to cause pain or threat

Thus, it is no surprise that in our own spiritual walk with God, the greatest position that the enemy likes to put us into is a state of fear. Our relationship with God isn't necessarily the thing that scares the enemy. Rather, it is when we get ahold of our mission that the enemy becomes terrified in his boots. When we realize that we are called to make disciples and step into the giftings that God has given us, it gets the attention of our adversary. When we step outside our comfort zone and do the very thing that has us paralyzed, the plot turns and the enemy then becomes a hostage of fear. As Christians, we have nothing to fear, because we know that we walk with the One who makes us victorious. Our faith is the antonym for our fear. When faith becomes all-consuming in our lives, it awakens us to a higher calling. Fear keeps us in a cage, while faith sets us free to follow after our God-given dreams, placed there by the One who created us.

When I first became an Indie Author, I had no idea what to expect. In the initial launch of each book, my mind began to overthink everything. Would anyone even buy it? Would people even enjoy it? Would people hate it? Oh, gosh, people are going to be reading a book with my name on it. What am I thinking? No, take it off the shelves. This is crazy. Please, someone talk me out of this. How do people do this?

In the writing of this book, I dealt with so much fear and opposition as I worked through the words that I felt led to share. As I wrestled with whether or not I should even publish this book for others to read, I realized that I had to overcome every thought that was trying to keep my giftings to myself. God's soft nudges kept pushing me to do the one thing that I knew I had been called to do: write.

While you may not be called to ever write a book one day, I guarantee you that there have been many times when you have felt not qualified for the work of God, where you look at all of your past mistakes and allow guilt to be the very thing that drives your next decision, instead of seeing yourself as God sees you. As a born-again Christian, you have been called out and chosen by God to carry out His mission. Thus, we have to be careful with what we consume and feed our minds with, for the thoughts that we choose to marinate on give power over the direction for our lives.

So, when it came to my writing, I took the plunge. I published my first book in 2017 and was scared out of my mind. As people started reading Unkempt Secrets from The War and asked me when I would write another book, those initial feelings of fear and anticipation were replaced with joy and excitement. I took a deep breath and relaxed. But, not for long.

I got my first negative review. As soon as I did, I wanted to take the book off the shelves. I wished I had never written it in the first place and asked myself, "What were you thinking, Jennifer? You? A writer?" And, then, I began flipping through the book and noticed an error that a friend had pointed out to me and right then and there, I wanted to quit. I was in the middle of writing A Song for Somme, and wanted to throw that project down the drain, too. That's when it hit me.

Isn't this just like the enemy? He will pinpoint one error or one mistake that we make in either our lives or the lives of others, which then makes us cancel out "the entire book" which is a metaphor for someone else's character or our own. If we aren't careful, we can entertain that one thought that points to that one flaw, that one inconsistency, that one thing that I do not like about myself or another, and then allow it to cancel out everything that we or they have worked so hard for.

"For we all stumble in many ways. If anyone does not stumble in what he says, he is a perfect man, able to bridle the whole body as well."
-James 3:2

Be careful as to what thoughts you invite into your life. **Uninvited thoughts will leave you at a dead end where you will believe more in social media's perfect agenda to have it all together rather than in the agenda of the One who says,** *My grace is sufficient for you.*
So, this is what I did. I surrendered my writing to God. I let Him rid of the fear that had me paralyzed from writing another word. The negative thoughts began to fade as I focused, instead, on my purpose to move forward with this gift. In the midst of negative thoughts, there was one thought that had power to overrule all the others. God's still small voice asked me, "Why do you write? And, who are you writing for?"

Sitting in my apartment, at the Midnight hour, I pulled open my journal and wrote down every reason for why I write, of which one of those reasons stood out above the rest. I write to bring hope, even if it's just one life. In writing my second novel A Song for Somme, which follows one atheist's journey towards belief in God, it has proved to be a tool to share about my faith and reach people in a very creative way. I have been able to share about God's love and redemption with people that I would have never had the chance to otherwise. If I had allowed fear to get its way, then you probably wouldn't be holding this book in your hands today. We were all created with different giftings to serve one purpose: to make the name of Jesus known. Don't allow negative thoughts to deter you from ever using your giftings.

When we overcome those negative thoughts, we can step into the life God has for us, a life that is able to bring hope to others, even if it's just one life. There will always be negative voices in our lives, but we have to learn to silence those unwanted voices.

So, today, I pray that God will help you to let go of those fearful thoughts. I pray that every negative emotion that is trying to tell you that you aren't enough or have what it takes to be used by God will be demolished by the Truth of God's Word that reveals in Christ alone, you are enough. As we go about each day and face many different thoughts, we carry something within us that God wants us to activate. The best way that you can fight the battles of your mind is to pick up your sword, The Word of God. We do not read the Word of God just to be inspired. We read it to be transformed and equipped for whatever battles this life has to offer. Hebrews 4: 12 states, "For the word of God *is* living and powerful, and sharper than any two-edged sword, piercing even to the division of soul and spirit, and of joints and marrow, and is a discerner of the thoughts and intents of the heart."

The Word of God is sharper than any two-edged sword. That's a pretty sharp sword, if you ask me. It's more powerful than any thought that tries to deter us away from God's plan.

JENNIFER MALECH

19

COUNT EVERY BLESSING

"God surpasses our dreams when we reach past our personal plans and agenda to grab the hand of Christ and walk the path He chose for us. He is obligated to keep us dissatisfied until we come to Him and His plan for complete satisfaction."
-Beth Moore

We can so often be looking for God to answer the big prayers that we don't even notice the little blessings all around us. God beckons us to take notice of the small things, for when we turn our attention towards Him and away from our problems and unanswered prayers, we will notice that God is in our midst even when it seems otherwise.

If you woke up this morning and have breath in your lungs, consider that a great blessing. If you woke up with the revelation of the name of Jesus and are able to utter those words without fear for your life, count this as great joy.

We read in the Psalms that when David was facing his enemies, he learned how to continually praise God, despite what his situation looked like. Sometimes, all it takes is lifting our eyes away from our situation and focusing, instead, on the many blessings that we do have, such as a roof over our heads, food on our tables, and the freedom to live in a nation where we can freely gather together and worship God.

We praise God not for what He's done or for what our circumstances are, but simply for who He is. Even when we are downcast, when we choose to fixate our eyes on Him, we have something to rejoice about.

Last year, I was put in a situation that was beyond my own comprehension. To spare the details, I had to leave a family situation for my own protection. Without anywhere to go, I pulled onto a street in a neighborhood and began to cry my eyes out. It was late in the night and I was absolutely terrified and heartbroken. As I sat in my car, the words from the song Waymaker played in the background. I could barely sing the words and as I tried to believe them, my heart felt shattered in ways that I had never known was possible. As I cried and tried to make sense of what to do next, I felt prompted to read Psalm 23. As I began to read the words out loud, I felt the power of the Holy Spirit in such a mighty way. With tears still streaming down my face, I began to declare the words of the psalm and felt the power of God in a way that I had never experienced before. I shouted the words as though God had written them specifically for me in that moment.

"The LORD *is* my shepherd;
I shall not want.
He makes me to lie down in green pastures;
He leads me beside the still waters.
He restores my soul;
He leads me in the paths of righteousness
For His name's sake.
Yea, though I walk through the valley of the shadow of death,
I will fear no evil;
For You *are* with me;
Your rod and Your staff, they comfort me.
You prepare a table before me in the presence of my enemies;
You anoint my head with oil;
My cup runs over.

Surely goodness and mercy shall follow me
All the days of my life;
And I will dwell in the house of the LORD
Forever."

When I said the last word, "forever," I felt the assurance of God's voice in that car. The following day, I wrote words in my journal that brought so much freedom in my mind. When I first shared these raw words with a dear friend of mine, she immediately texted me back and said, "Jen, maybe this is what this season is all about. I hope you share these words in a book someday." So, Amy, you were right. I'm going to share these words in a book one day and that day is today.

"Last night, as I was praying and crying out to God, I felt God remind me, "David wrote this when he was running from his enemies, just as you are now. You are choosing to declare praise in the middle of your pain. If David had never faced such pain, you wouldn't have this moment to declare the promise." David's pain all those years ago was used to minister to a girl crying in her car in the 21st century. That's what God does. He takes those moments of misunderstanding and chooses to change our perspective so that we may learn the power of who our God is. Just as Paul was in the prison cell, I'm sure he was like, "God, I'm serving you! Why would you let me end up here?" But, instead of choosing that to be his focus, he chose to praise God. That is our reference for how we should live our Christian lives. So, in the midst of the pain, I am choosing to do that right now."

When God reminded me of what David had to walk through to bring comfort to me in that frightening hour, I felt like having a praise break right there in the neighborhood. But, it was in the middle of the night, so I didn't want to cause disruption at that hour. Although, what a story that could have been. You see, I was just so overwhelmed by the love of God that reaches out to us and reminds us that no pain is wasted. Over the course of those months, the pain would come and go, but I continued to choose to worship God and trust that

God would use my own pain to bring glory to His name. God used the lowest season in my life so that His goodness and mercy could be declared among others.

In that dark season, I continually discovered that complete satisfaction is found through the love of Jesus Christ. We will always be disappointed and led astray when we place our hope and our trust elsewhere. That night, I put my hope in Jesus and knew that in my surrender to Him, every broken thing would be used so that others may come to know Jesus and be filled with hope, too.

Today, everything in your world may be in turmoil, but God will see you through it. His peace surpasses all understanding. Right now, I pray that the joy of the LORD would flood your room or wherever you are as you read these words right now. As I write this devotional, I am listening to a song that I grew up listening to and I want to share it with all of you here.

"Better is one day in your courts,
Better is one day in your house,
Better is one day in your courts,
Than thousand elsewhere."

I would encourage you to put this song on and take a moment to just worship God. We have nothing to fear in the presence of the LORD. We have full access to joy in the presence of our God. There is nothing more beautiful than this truth. Thank you, Jesus, that we get to call on your name. What a gift it is that He hears us when we call on His name.

"In my distress I called upon the LORD,
And cried out to my God;
He heard my voice from His temple,
And my cry came before Him, *even* to His ears.
                                        -Psalm 18:6

20

THE GREATEST LOVE OF ALL

"He is Light, Living Water, the Path to God, a Shepherd
seeking lost sheep. He is life itself. He told compelling stories,
and He is the story...He called us to follow, to experience life
like never before, to share with others in the life of faith.
Passion, meaning, imagery, experience. Each of those has
tremendous meaning for an evangelist; each one is part of the
good news of the gospel."
-Leonard Sweet

Love is a choice, not a feeling. Love is self-sacrifice beyond
our own understanding. Love is giving without expecting
anything in return. Love is driving two hours out of your way
to have dinner with a friend who had a really hard day. Love is
doing the hard things, the behind the scene things that no one
else wants to do. Love is taking someone by the hand and
staying with them in the middle of their mess. Love is getting
up in the middle of the night when you get that unexpected
phone call. Love is not thinking of yourself at all, but thinking
about how you can better serve others. Love is saying yes when
it would be easier to say no. Love is oh so patient.
    When Jesus died on a cross, He showed us the deepest
form of love. He died, not knowing if we would love Him in

return.

A few years ago, a thought had entered my mind. "It's scary to care so much for someone when it's quite possible that they don't care for you as much or at all." And, something tugged at my spirit when I felt God whisper, "I know this all too well. So is my love for so many people." Wow. This hit me hard.

Jesus died on a cross not knowing if we would choose Him in return. God's love is seen so beautifully through the story of the prodigal son. Even when his son walked away, the father would wait every day, hoping that his son would return. Even through the hurt and pain, he waited. And, when his son returned, he ran towards him, clothed him in the finest robe and threw his son a party.

"'I will set out and go back to my father and say to him: Father, I have sinned against heaven and against you. I am no longer worthy to be called your son; make me like one of your hired servants.' So he got up and went to his father. But while he was still a long way off, his father saw him and was filled with compassion for him; he ran to his son, threw his arms around him and kissed him."
-Luke 15:18-20

Even when we walk away or make mistakes, Jesus stands at the door waiting for us. And, when we return, Jesus doesn't scold us, but He rejoices. He throws a party! This love goes beyond our understanding, but this is how Jesus loves us and demonstrates to us how we should love others.

God manifested himself in human flesh and lived a life that would guarantee that you and I could experience true love. We are undeserving of this love, yet he gives it freely and if we accept, we will come to experience the greatest gift here on earth. If you are in a season where you are feeling shame or guilt for something you have done and this is keeping you from entering fully into what God has in store for you, please know that Jesus is beckoning you back into His house. His love is an invitation to everyone, no matter who you are. Jesus is eagerly waiting for you to run towards Him. He doesn't look at where you have been, but looks at where you are going as He wraps you up with His robe, a robe made possible because of His true love. Jesus is wanting to throw you a party. There is nothing that we have to do, but repent. He wants us to turn around from the direction we've been trying to walk in all on our own. God looks forward to us returning back to the Father's house. In our own humility, we are able to accept the gift that He is so eagerly wanting to give us: forgiveness. Through the brokenness and past mistakes, God is welcoming you back into His arms so that He can refine you into gold, so pure.

GOLD, SO PURE.

it's something new
at least, that is how i feel
in these years
that i have known you

it cannot be explained
how you have
pressed me into your palm
with love
that gives no conditions

i am hopeful
i am joyful
i am free

it's something new
at least, that is what I know
after these months
that I have struggled

it cannot be explained
how you have picked me up
taken everything broken
and, refined it
into gold, so pure.

i am thankful
i am happy
i am free

it's something new
at least, that is what I believe
after all this time
that i have wandered

i am overwhelmed
i am dancing in the kitchen
i am smiling
with this gift you've given me

so sweet, so pure
you've made me see
there is purpose in the pain
for redemption, I would not know
you turn the brokenness
into gold, so pure.

had it not been
for all the wrestling

we never would have
ended up here

oh, we never would have
ended up here
gold, so pure
only you knew
all this time
all along
your love was making
something new.

JENNIFER MALECH

21

TENDING THE WILDFLOWERS

"If God gives such attention to the appearance of wildflowers-
most which are never even seen-don't you think he'll attend to
you, take pride in you, do his best for you? What I'm trying to
do here is to get you to relax, to not be so preoccupied with
getting, so you can respond to God's giving…Steep your life in
God reality, God initiative, God-provisions."
-Matthew 6:30-33 MSG

Have you ever walked through a field of wildflowers? It's
simply wonderful. There's something so wonderful about
wandering through a wide-open flower field, and wearing
flowers in your hair. I would totally wear a flower crown every
day if I could, but I opt for hats, instead. It could be my
bohemian style or the fact that my choice of music usually
includes some form of the banjo, or that I love healthy foods,
whatever it is, my friends have often called me a flower child.
I'll take it.

All of this to say, I really love wildflowers, the way they
emerge in their own element, unique in color and scent. I think
each of us are at our best when we emerge in our own element,
and don't get distracted or weighed down by comparison of
those around us. Freedom comes in the mind when we stop

comparing our lives with those around us.

God takes great care of the wildflowers. He tends to them and takes pride in His creation, just as He does you and I. He doesn't want you to look around to try to be someone else or become consumed by worry that you will lose supply of food and water just to stay alive. Just as a field of wildflowers is tended to and taken care of by God, so are you. If God can take care of the wildflowers, even those that are hidden and forgotten in the depth of the forest, then what makes us think that He won't provide to meet our needs?

Shortly after graduating from college and moving out on my own, I hit a lot of financial trouble. If you have graduated college, I am sure you are nodding your head right now and know exactly what I am talking about. The grace period for my loans was over and the bills were stacking up pretty high, while all the meanwhile I was trying to figure out how I would keep myself fed. After paying my tithes, rent, and all my bills for that month, I had completely emptied out my Checking account. I had just enough money to get me to and from work, and wondered what a week of eating Bear Grylls style would look like. To be honest, I don't think that would have even been possible here in Los Angeles. Needless to say, I was feeling pretty low, but then I remembered the promise in Matthew 6. God takes care of the wildflowers, so won't He take care of me? The following day at church, a friend placed a card in my purse. When I got in my car, I found it and opened it up. There was a $50 Trader Joe's Gift Card. I would have groceries for the week. You better believe I started crying right then and there in that car. This is only one of many stories of how God has continually provided in my life. And, I am certain that if you and I sat across the table from one another, sipping on our coffee of choice, you would tell me all the times that God has been faithful to you and your family, too. My pastor's wife, Tamara Brown, has told our church on multiple occasions, **"If you take care of God's business, He will take care of yours."** This principle is so true. Take care of God's house and He will take care of your house.

Sometimes, we feel that God may not hear or see us in this large world, but the reality is He is omnipresent and omnipotent. Sometimes, we have to remind ourselves of that. He deeply cares about us and sees us right where we are.

Our God is the One who performs the miraculous, the same God who fed 5,000 with five loaves of bread and two fish from the sea. We are finite and our human minds can't comprehend fully what our God is capable of, but we must remember to relax our muscles as we gaze out at the ocean waves. Breathe in the salty air and allow yourself to be emerged in the promises of His goodness.

He tends the wildflowers, He feeds the fish in the sea, He takes care of the cattle, He provides rain when there is a drought, He provides oxygen to the land through the plants of this earth. He knows and sees all, what an overwhelming thought this can be. And, somehow, He sees us, He knows us, He longs for our hearts, and He tends to our every need. If our earthly father seeks to provide for us, or whomever is a guardian in your life, how much more will our heavenly father provide for us?

Go to God in prayer. It is our lifeline, our oxygen tank. "Your Father knows the things you have need of before you ask Him." Matthew 6:8.

A father who selflessly loves his children will go to great heights to make sure they are provided for. God so selflessly loves us that He went to extreme heights by robing Himself in flesh here on earth and then dying for our sins so that we may not only experience the greatest gift of salvation, but so that we may also experience earthly blessings and favor through covenant relationship with Him.

JENNIFER MALECH

22

HIS PLAN, THE BEST PLAN

"You can make many plans, but the Lord's purpose will
prevail."
-Proverbs 19:21

As human beings, we inevitably have a plethora of dreams,
hopes and goals for our future. We look towards the great
unknown and wonder where our lives will end up. We look
ahead and visualize the future that is to take place. We are
planners.

There are times in our lives when a situation takes place and
it didn't turn out as we had hoped or dreamed. And, we sit for
a moment, take a deep breath and wonder why and how we
ended up where we are at right now. However, The Lord's
purpose will always prevail.

"Let us fix our eyes on Jesus, the author and perfecter of our
faith, who for the joy set before Him endured the cross,
scorning its shame and sat down at the right hand of the
throne of God." Hebrews 12:2

There is one thing that we can intend on always doing and it is simply this: fix our eyes on Jesus. When we learn to fixate our eyes on Jesus, our situations become mere images in our rearview mirror as we begin to recognize and understand that God is leading us down the road towards His greater purpose. There is no need in looking back at what could have been or what I could have done differently. Looking towards the past won't move you forward in life.

Oftentimes, we wonder why we went through a certain storm or why did a particular situation not turn out as we had hoped. **The fact is that sometimes, the storm was necessary to get you to where God wants to take you.** Storms often get our attention to reach upwards towards heaven and rely solely on Jesus Christ to guide us through it all.

When you come out of a difficult or challenging circumstance, you grow. Trials turn into testimonies. We sometimes think that it is better to seek comfort instead of friction. We want life to go according to our own perfect plan, but if that was the case, we wouldn't truly be living a life built on trust in God, now would we? **Uncomfortable roads lead to life's greatest growth.**

A couple years ago, I had the wonderful opportunity of traveling to England with one of my dear friends. We spent ten days traveling all throughout the beautiful country, three of those days spent driving through the country roads of Cornwall. This beautiful part of the country is located about four hours southwest of London. For those who have never traveled to England, you may not be aware that in England, they drive on the left side of the road. To make matters even more complicated, the driver's seat is on the opposite side as we Americans know. Uncomfortable, to say the least.

As though that wasn't difficult enough, our GPS died 30 minutes outside the airport which forced me to read a real map, ladies and gentlemen. Neither of us had purchased International cell service for this trip. More than that, though, when driving through the countryside of Cornwall, the roads were so narrow to where one car could barely fit, and mind you, these little country roads were two-way! So, needless to say, it was a little uncomfortable. My dear friend, Samantha, was a champ, though. She conquered those roads like she had been driving them all her life. We did call upon the name of Jesus, though, a few times. But, we made it out alive. All is well.

Now, when our GPS first died 30 minutes outside London, I was not a happy camper. Poor Sam had to gently deal with my initial outburst of anger. As the rain beat on and we drove past hundreds of sheep wandering amongst the beautiful green hillside, I closed my eyes and took a deep breath. Through the anger, all I could think about was the fact that now we would not be able to explore the cities we had plan on seeing that day. All of our careful planning had gone completely out the window. And, now, we had to find somewhere with free WiFi so that we could pull up the map coordinates of our AirBnB which of course was not located on the little map I had held in the palm of my hands. I had thought our entire road trip to Cornwall was ruined. As I continued to stare out the window, I let out another deep breath and made a choice. It honestly took me about twenty minutes to regain my composure. But, when I did, everything clicked. I realized that I had been so focused on my plan that when things didn't go accordingly, I was allowing it to negatively determine the way that I behaved and chose to enjoy the rest of the trip. Sound familiar? We do this more often than we like.

So, right then and there, I made a decision. Although, in that moment, I had no idea if we were to arrive at our Cornwall cottage by nightfall, and though I was disappointed that now we wouldn't be able to cross off cities and sights off our itinerary list, I realized that it was all part of the journey. The fact of the matter is that we had created an itinerary, and while our itinerary didn't quite go according to plan, in the end, it ended up being better than we could have hoped. We have to accept that there will be things on our life itinerary that we will never be able to check off the list. Life won't always go according to plan, yet we have been given the choice on whether or not we will surrender our plans over to God. And, let me tell you, when you surrender your plans and truly let go, you will live with more peace and freedom in your heart that trusts God has everything under control. Yes, it is good to have a plan, but don't be so focused on it that you miss what God is wanting to do. Had our GPS not died, we would have never had the joys of traveling down roads less traveled. Had our GPS not died, we would have never gone to places that were never on our itinerary to begin with.

Now, I know this story is a very lighthearted example of things not going according to plan, but I think it puts into perspective the more difficult road blocks we face in this life. And, in the midst of your difficult circumstances, small or grand, will you focus on the situation or will you choose to place your trust in The Situation Maker, the God who knows the beginning from end? When we focus on what is instead of what could have been, we will more freely be able to enjoy a life of true contentment.

We have a plan. God has an even better plan. Go to God in the secret place. Seek His will and when you seek Him, you will find peace knowing that God's plan is the best plan for our lives. Psalm 20:7 states, "Some trust in chariots and some in horses, but we will remember the name of the Lord our God."

Even if you can't see it right now, know that God has a greater purpose in it. Each circumstance in your life is teaching you to be more like Christ, but the choice is entirely yours. Will you fixate your eyes on Jesus in all circumstances? Will you allow His plan to be the best plan for your life?

23

THE PRUNING PROCESS

"Embrace the pruning and the sacrifice to get where God wants to take you. It's going to hurt. But, it's going to create greater understanding."
-Drew Keatts

Each circumstance in our life produces character. We get to determine how we will respond to the chapters of our lives. There is room for growth in each season of our lives and we get to decide whether or not we will be molded by God's pen or our own. If we are to step into God's purpose for our lives, we must be refined in our own lives to become more like Christ. By no means it is an easy process, but it is absolutely necessary for what God is wanting to do in and through you. This is God's heart towards the pruning process: we must become broken and humbled in order to step into God's destiny for our lives. Will it hurt? Yes. But, it is necessary for where God wants to take you. It requires a process.

A couple years ago, David Gettys taught a message during our midweek service that made such an impact on my life. In his message, he said, "What you are going through isn't going to take you down, it's going to take you up. God says, when I can look at you through the fiery trials and see my image reflected, I can use you."

When we go back to the very beginning of biblical text, we see how God first took his people through a process, a process that sometimes looked like a bit of a wrestling match. But, the pain was necessary because by it, God put something within man that allowed him to bear His image.

The pruning process can be better defined as the sanctification process. The process of sanctification is absolutely necessary for where God wants to take you and what He is wanting to do in and through you. There are things in your life that God is trying to rid of so that you can step into the promises that He has for your life. Sometimes, we have to become broken in order for us to recognize that our strength does not come from our own abilities or skills, but it comes from placing our trust in God's power.

When I first stepped into leadership, I became so burnt out and so frustrated when it seemed that all of my efforts were getting nowhere. It took a hard fall for me to realize that I was relying on my own strength and trying to do things my own way. God gently asked me, "Did you ever seek me on that decision?" I quickly realized that I was making decisions and judgements based on what I thought was best. I was trying to prove myself to Him, rather than letting Him prove Himself to me. I was allowing my own human gifts to become a substitute for the power and direction of His Spirt. And, let me tell you. There is no substitute for God's Holy Spirit. If you try to do things by your own strength, no matter how talented and gifted you are, you'll miss the true heartbeat of God. Scripture tells us in Matthew 6 to seek first the Kingdom. We must seek God through daily devotion. Without a personal relationship with God, we will not grow into what He wants us to be, but into the image that we think is best for our lives. That is a dangerous place to be. When we begin to rely on our own giftings and think that it is by our own effort that we will see the fruit of our labor, we better check our heart pulse, because it might very well be that our hearts are beating with pride. Through different circumstances in my own life, I have seen how pride has always gotten in the way of what God wants to do. But, thank goodness for His loving discipline and correction. The process of sanctification helped remove pride in my own life so that I could be His pride.

Sanctification is absolutely necessary for where God wants to take you. When we begin to truly seek God, He will shift our mindsets, remove the filth that has taken residence for too long, and reveal to us His heartbeat through His Word. When we are molded into His image, we don't try to do things our own way with our own abilities and skills, but we give over those abilities and skills to Him, realizing that His Spirit within us gives us the wisdom and strength to do the task at hand. There is so much power available to us through the Holy Spirit! We just have to get out of the way.

Oswald Chambers once wrote, "Sanctification is not drawing from Jesus the power to be holy-it is drawing from Jesus the very holiness that was exhibited in Him, and that He now exhibits in me. Sanctification is an impartation, not an imitation. Imitation is something altogether different. The perfection of everything is in Jesus Christ, and the mystery of sanctification is that all the perfect qualities of Jesus are at my disposal. Consequently, I slowly but surely begin to live a life of inexpressible order, soundness, and holiness, kept by the power of God."

This is why daily prayer is absolutely vital, because by it, we discover God's heartbeat, and find direction for our lives. Through prayer, we allow our hearts to be changed and molded by God. We become image bearers of Christ as we begin to possess His qualities, something that happens when we consecrate and devote ourselves to Him. It will require a new level in sacrifice as you seek to live a life that reflects His holiness.

It may very well be that God may use the most broken chapter of your life not only to sift some things out of your life, but also to impart some things into your life. The most important key to remember in all of this is that none of this is ours. It all belongs to God.

The difficult chapters that you have walked through are worth it when you give your life to Jesus, because every painful chapter will be used to reveal His glory and help others on their own journey. If it hadn't been for a very difficult few years, the words in this book would have never been written. Don't detest the season you are in. With Jesus, He wants to do incredible things through your life and let this world know that He is the answer they are searching for.

24

TRUST WITHOUT BORDERS

"God doesn't want something from us. He simply wants us."
-C.S. Lewis

"Trusting God without seeing solutions is hard. But that's the
fertile soil where faith grows."
-Lysa Terkeurst

There are times in our life that are more difficult than
others. It is in those seasons that God gives us a new
perspective so that we may be able to gain a hold of His vision.
Trusting in God is an everyday decision that requires a strength
outside of ourselves, a strength that comes when we lean not
on our own strength, but on His, instead. When your
circumstances are frustrating and seem too impossible to ever
find a solution, that is when you place your hope in a God who
truly does care about what you are walking through and where
you are headed. **In seasons of difficulty, we discover whose
strength we are truly leaning on.** This dependency on
ourselves, which is rooted in our independent culture, goes

against God's desire to place our full trust in Him. God is beckoning us to trust Him fully, to depend not on our strength, but in His alone.

Trust is the foundation in our relationship with God, as much, and if not more, than our relationship with one another.

It is easy to trust God when everything's going smoothly, but what about when you just lost your job, when the doctor's report is negative, or when an unexpected situation happens in your home? Is your trust unwavering, even then?

Our trust in God should be a trust that is without borders, a trust that knows God has us in the palms of His hands. When we understand that our lives belong to Christ, then we understood that every circumstance, good and bad, belongs to Him. Keep your eyes fixated on Him, even in the unseen. Your greatest testimony is being birthed in the unseen. I mentioned this verse at the very start of this book, one that I have taped to my bathroom mirror, reminding me of this very truth. If I could give this entire book a theme verse, if would be 2 Corinthians 4:18. "So we fix our eyes not on what is seen, but what is unseen, since what is seen is temporary, but what is unseen is eternal."

Have you ever flown on an airplane before? Well, if you have, then you know that feeling of having to place a lot of trust in the pilot of the big jet. I mean, if you really think about it, you are placing your trust in someone that you don't know. All you know is that he or she earned their wings and is the one in charge of getting you to your destination. I mean, you hoped he or she earned their wings.

One day, I was having a conversation with a friend about flying. If you must know, it was my dream to go into aviation as a career since I was a little girl. Somewhere around 16, I decided that maybe that wasn't the best route for me. My fascination with flying began when my grandfather would take my brother and I to the Salinas Air Show. We spent every year walking around the airfield, learning about all the different airplanes, and enjoyed watching the airshow from our box seats where we would watch The Blue Angels and my favorite, the Stealth, take to the sky. It was simply marvelous. It still is.

So, as my friend and I were talking about flying, she told me that she is terrified of flying across the ocean. Her reason: There is just so much unknown when flying over such a large body of water. As I thought about it, it made sense. When flying, a lot of people feel most safe when they can see the ground beneath them, but as soon as the land disappears, there is this great feeling of despair. But, if we truly trust the pilot knows what he/she is doing, even when there is no sign of life that catches our attention from where we sit miles above air, then we can relax into our seats and know that it's going to be okay. We will arrive where we need to safely because the pilot can see what we can't from where we sit as passengers. Thus, if we are to fly out into the unknown, we have to believe that the One in charge of the airplane of our lives truly knows what He is doing.

Do you remember the first airplane ride you went on? How nervous were you? By your twentieth flight, I guarantee that you weren't as nervous as the very first time you ever boarded an airplane. The more that we entrust our life to God as the pilot of our lives, the easier it will become to trust God with the unseen parts of our life, that which we do not know lies ahead of us. Of course, for some, your twentieth flight is just as nerve-wrecking as your first flight, and that is okay, too. Yet, even amidst the nerves, when flying above the clouds, you can't help but take a moment to marvel at how incredible it is to see life in a new way that you wouldn't have been able to had you remained on the ground. When you learn to let go of control, you are able to see life from a new perspective, a perspective that gives you access into the unseen.

JENNIFER MALECH

25

PEACH MILKSHAKES
AND OPEN DOORS

"It was on the other side of a closed door that a divine dream
began to come to shape."
-Travis Worthington

"I have opened a door for you that no man can close."
Revelation 3:8

I was sitting across from a friend, who was walking through
a tough season, a season where she was questioning God's
purpose in the pain. I sat there and listened. It wasn't the first
time we had been having this conversation. It had been
months of showing up for one another, and staying when the
tears became heavy. There were nights where she would cry on
my couch and I would hold her, reminding her that God is
going to complete what He had already started in her, even if
we couldn't understand it in that moment. And, when the tears
had subsided, we were able to take a deep breath together and
find whatever beauty we could in the day. On one of those
particular days, we had ended up at Chick-fil-A for milkshakes,
because when it's in the 100s in Southern California, you better

believe ice cream is always the best answer. When is ice cream not a good idea? I don't care if it's below freezing outside, ice cream is still a good idea.

So, we sat across from one another, and after taking another one of those deep breaths, we smiled at one another and I said, "Sometimes, life is tough, but then there is always time for peach milkshakes." In the midst of not knowing what would come next, we reminded one another that God has our best interest at heart. And, in the middle of the pain, He is reshaping our dreams and our heartbeat to align with His. As my friend Charity once shared on a podcast we had done together, "There is purpose in the pain we walk through."

When God closes one door, He opens an even better one. Knocking on God's door doesn't mean that the door will answer according to our own expectations. Rather, knocking on God's door means that He is always on the other side of my fervent knocking. We aren't in this alone.

While He knows the desires of my heart, God also knows what door will lead to His divine promises. Sometimes it takes closed doors in order for these promises to come to take place in our lives. God wants us to keep knocking on His door even when things don't go according to our plan. And, He wants us to keep knocking for the friends in our lives who are walking through painful chapters, too.

Keep trusting in God. The definition of trust means to have a firm reliability and confidence in someone else. In no way can I be confident in my own abilities, but I can be confident in His. Days, months or years later, we will come to the realization as to why that door had been shut. If that door had not been closed (painful childhood experiences, negative medical report, loss of a job, breakup, etc.), then we would not be where we are today.

Isaiah 55:8-9 states, "For My thoughts are not your thoughts, nor are your ways My ways," says the LORD. For as the heavens are higher than the earth,
So are My ways higher than your ways,
And My thoughts than your thoughts."

God will open a new door in your life, a door of opportunity that could have never been opened to you had you not walked through the hard stuff. In the meantime, as you wait for God's purpose to unfold in your life, pull up a chair, and order yourself a peach milkshake.

HELD.

there is more danger
in pretending
it's alright
than allowing yourself
to recognize
that sometimes
it's okay
not to be okay

sometimes,
it takes everything
inside of us
to whisper to God
as we try
to hold it together
and, that's okay

Let yourself be held, friend
Surrender your emotions
And, hide yourself
Under the shadow
Of His wings
Where you don't have to depend
On your own strength

26

DEAR CHILD OF DIVORCE

"As my sufferings mounted I soon realized that there were two
ways in which I could respond to my situation—either to react
with bitterness or seek to transform the suffering into a
creative force. I decided to follow the latter course."
-Martin Luther King Jr.

You might have read the title of this particular devotion
and may feel as though this chapter does not apply to you, but
I want to say that whoever you are, whether a child of divorce
or not, I wrote this chapter for you. Because the fact of the
matter is, whether or not you yourself are a child of such
circumstances, you know someone who is. As someone who
has worked in ministry, I have found how important it is to
learn and understand more about human character and
development, especially when someone has faced trauma of
various kinds. By learning about what happens to the human
mind when different tragedies take place in the home, such as
divorce, the loss of a loved one, etc, we are better able to find
sympathy for one another. We are better able to understand
how we can pray for one another when we come to learn how
certain circumstances affects our hearts and minds. Now, I had

never planned to write this chapter. In fact, it was added after I printed the first proof of this book before publication. While going through the final edit, I felt the gentle nudge to write this chapter. Unfortunately, I know of young people who have had to face this most recently and my heart broke, knowing the emotions that they were walking through. And, while I wish I didn't know what it's like to have one's parents go through a divorce, I thanked God that He was able to use the dysfunction that I came from to minister to these teenagers in their time of need.

Because of what we have had to face throughout our lives, God gives us a greater understanding on how we can better pray for others when they are walking through their own pain. God uses our own scars to minister and bring healing into other people's lives through both a place of empathy and compassion. Whatever your story is, God will use the brokenness that has occurred in your own life to help bring mending into another person's life. That is just what God does. John 14:27 states, "Peace I leave with you, my peace I give to you; not as the world gives do I give to you. Let not your heart be troubled, neither let it be afraid."

So, this letter is to all of the children whose homes have been uprooted. This letter is for the adults who are trying to help understand how these children are feeling. And, this is for the person who will receive insight on how they can better pray for families and children who come from divorced homes. This is the letter that I wish I had read when I was 14. I shared it on a blogpost a little over a year ago, but want to share it here, as well.

Dear Child of Divorce,

I know where you've been and I know right now where you stand. Through it all, be reminded of this: You are strong. You don't have the answers and that is okay. And, you are not alone.

Your heart will always long for a mother and father under one roof. Even years after your heart has been healed, there will still be moments where it is okay to cry. In the midst of your pain, may you know that you are being refined into a pillar of compassion. Though most of it doesn't make sense, know that you are being held in the arms of Yahweh, who is both mother and father, who understands your beating heart in ways that no one else can.

Life will not be easy. In fact, life isn't easy for anyone, but you bear a unique burden that is often not known by the world you walk through. You can't explain to the streets you step on that you live your life constantly caught in the middle, thrust between homes with a tension that never ceases.

Celebrations are jovial, but they also bring about grief, for the reminder that one home became two, and that on that desired forgotten day, your heart broke in half. The shadow of divorce is present at graduations, weddings, momentous occasions of various kinds.

Wounds once healed will be opened again. And, while you try to be quiet, and tell the world that you are just fine, know this: it's okay not to always be strong.

Yet, in those moments, where life becomes numb, and your world feels as though it's no longer your own, be reminded that there is a promise that all things will be redeemed. Caught in the middle, you may never feel that you are enough for your parents. To please one is to dismay another, but do not be grieved by this sobering reality. Because even as you seek both their approval, but seem to never find it fully, know that you are enough.

Not because of who you are, but because of who God is. Even if you fall wayward, you are His beloved. You don't have to prove yourself. You don't have to listen to lies. You don't have to measure up to anyone else's standards. You don't have to be afraid to love. You don't have to give up hope on marriage or having a family of your own one day. In Christ alone, you are enough.

Healing comes in time. It will get easier, though there will be nights where inevitable tears remind you of the words that haunt your memory, "We are getting a divorce."

Let your life not be full of bitterness, but gratefulness for the breath you take, day by day. Let your life be used to bring glory to God. Let the pain be turned into art and creativity that silences the enemy and gives honor to God, who redeems even the messiest of situations. Let the unknown be turned into hope. And, let your heart know that not for one moment are you ever alone. You are stronger than you'll ever know.

With love and understanding,
A child of divorce.

DAY BY DAY

A wise man once said
Isn't it strange, funny rather
To feel as though day by day, nothing changes
Then, to look back
And, see just how much has changed

How right you are, Mr. C.S. Lewis

We live through moments
Sometimes, we go through the motions
Other times, we celebrate the motion
But, we live and love through moments
Moments that define us, shape us, mold us
And, ultimately, change us

Daylight disappears and suddenly,
These moments
Beautiful moments in time
Can shatter
Just as quickly
As they had become

Yet, through the good, bad and ugly
While I have changed
God has not.
God is the same yesterday, today and forever

Our thoughts, our actions, our dreams,
our plans, our days, our moments
They change
Sometimes they change just as quickly
as the waves beating the shore
Yet, God's plan is still the same

And, I feel my heart catching its breath
When I realize
It's good to trust
To trust with all my heart

To acknowledge God in every moment
To see the unseen
And, know that He has a far greater plan

Time goes
Life changes
Emotions fluctuate
Dreams are shattered
New hopes arise
And, again and again
Our breath meets the breath of God

He points to the waters
We see in our reflection
How much we've changed
Yet, how He has remained
Constant through the ages

We stand amazed
That He knew
All along

For, beauty arises from ashes
Anointing derives from pain

His plan
So beyond our understanding
Absolutely incomprehensible
Yet, intricately designed
Leads us down the right path
Towards everlasting life

His scars change us day by day
As we beat on with the dust

Each moment
Writes lyrics to our psalms

Psalms of both thanksgiving and lament
Where time has changed us
Yet, continually redeemed us

Day by day,
We run this race
Day by day,
We see how much has changed
And, then, we begin to kind of understand

The enigma
Of God's love
And, redemption plan
That invites you and I
To spread His love
Day by day

JENNIFER MALECH

27

TAKE THE WORLD, BUT GIVE ME JESUS

Take the world, but give me Jesus,
All its joys are but a name;
But His love abideth ever,
Through eternal years the same

Take the world, but give me Jesus
Sweetest comfort of my soul;
With my Saviour watching over me,
I can sing though billows roll

Though our circumstances may change, the truth of His goodness does not. Take the world, but give me Jesus. Worship is an expression of adoration for our King, an understanding that this world cannot offer what only Jesus alone can.

When I was in my Senior Seminar class at APU, Professor Hartwig looked at all of us eager students and asked us a question, "Can you look at your life and really say that Jesus is enough?" In a thought-provoking conversation that night, my heart was stirred. I think I can, I said to myself. Of course, I can. But, what I quickly realized is that this was a question that I would have to ask myself daily, because there would be seasons where I would try to fill my heart up with other things other than Jesus.

I believe God gives us dreams and desires, and while there is nothing wrong in our ambitions and successes, it is when our drive for success and control tries to fill us up that an alarm must be sounded. "For what profit is it to a man if he gains the whole world, but loses his soul?" -Matthew 16:26

If you also think of Toby Mac when you read that verse, then we grew up in the same generation. I was in middle school when my friends and I went to Spirit West Coast and listened to Toby Mac sing, "I don't want to gain the whole world, and lose my soul." It wasn't until I was an adult that I had to look myself in the mirror and ask, "Are you gaining the world right now? Who are you doing this for?"

Working as a writer in the Advertising Industry is a really interesting career. It's a career I stumbled upon, and it's actually a pretty crazy story. So, one day I will have to tell you about it. But, for now, I want to tell you a story about surrender. As I stepped into my career as a writer, I quickly realized how easy it is to become consumed and motivated by success. As I got sucked into the world of Advertising, and started going to Advertising School in my free time, working my way through amazing opportunities in my field, I had a wake-up call. My heart was completely in the wrong place. And, while there is nothing wrong with being successful in your career, it is when you are placing your fulfillment in your work that something needs to change. I realized that there was a part of me that was serving myself, instead of serving Him. What God began to reveal to me is that I hadn't fully surrendered my career over to Him. Whether you realize it or not, God requires that we surrender our education and our careers over to Him. If anything comes before God in our lives, it is an idol. When I realized my heart was motivated by the wrong thing, I decided to release and surrender my career over to Him. God is inviting you and I to surrender our dreams and desires over to Him, every last one of them.

Conviction still needs to be preached. Because, if it wasn't for the Holy Spirit and convicting messages from my pastor and other leaders in my life, I might have gotten so caught up in the glamour and lights of success that I would have become sidetracked from the mission. Does it mean that we have to give up our careers? No. But, God does require that we surrender our careers fully to Him. The reality is that God may call you to give up your career one day to go into the full-time ministry, but He also may never do that. What matters most is that as we work and take up different jobs, our careers are completely placed in His hands.

I don't remember the exact words, but one day, my pastor had shared with our church that **there will be a part of you that will be empty until you are doing what you are called to do.** Wherever you work, wherever you go to school, wherever you live, you are called to be His vessel of light. We are all missionaries, no matter what field we work in. We are called to be the church outside the four walls. Every day, you and I are called to ministry. What a beautiful invitation that is. We aren't in this alone. Let His Holy Spirit guide you in your everyday, let Him guide you to people who need His love.

I had to get to the point that if God asked me to give up my career that I love, that I would be okay with it. At first this was hard to grasp, because I love my career, but God continually revealed to me that in order to live for Him, all of my life has to be fully surrendered to Him. Success in His Kingdom looks so different from success according to the world's standards. God is requiring something more of us. He is calling us to a life of sacrifice and surrender.

To wrap this up, I want to share words from a song by Jimmy Needham. In his song, Clear the Stage, he reminds us of the importance of checking our hearts for anything in our lives that is put before God.

Anything I put before my God is an idol
Anything I want with all my heart is an idol
And anything I can't stop thinking of is an idol...

Worship is more than a song
Clear the stage and set the sound and lights ablaze
If that's the measure you must take to crush the idols.

Oh, the sweetness of Jesus. He is enough. He is all we could ever need. When our personal desires don't come to be, when the dreams never become a reality, when disappointment comes knocking at our door, when another day goes by and it seems that nothing has changed, when life feels mundane, when prayers go unanswered, He is still good. That is why we worship. It is in true worship, worship without reservation, worship without our own personal agenda, worship without a plan, worship without our flesh standing in the way, worship without distractions, that we come to know our King.

28

JAZZ+BLUEBERRIES

"Present means we understand that the here and now is sacred, sacramental, threaded through with divinity even in its plainness."
-Shauna Niequist

I live in the cutest part of Long Beach called Bixby Knolls, which truly reminds me a lot of Morgan Hill, the small American town where I spent a lot of my childhood. What I love about Bixby Knolls is that it is very family friendly, filled with a lot of outdoor activities for both kids and parents and single adults just wanting to have a good time and feel nostalgic about their childhood or something like that.

During the summer, my neighborhood puts on summer concerts in the park. It is wonderful fun. Everyone brings their blankets and chairs and sits out in the park to listen to the live band. I went a lot one summer, sometimes just casually strolling by to take a quick listen, and other times, I stayed for the entire concert, and even brought along my blanket and Trader Joe's dinner, which during summer months includes crackers, salami, cheese and fruit. Don't tell me I'm the only one.

On one of those particular days, I brought along someone who is dear to me. This family member struggles with depression, and to spare a lot of details of the situation, a couple hours filled with laughter together is a true and very rare gift from God. As I sat there, eating from the carton of blueberries and watched as this person's face filled with delight at the jazz music that serenaded us in the park, my heart felt as though it was about to explode. These moments between us are rare, and as the two of us belted out Natural Woman together in the park, I felt a smile spread across my face that no one would be able to wipe off even if they had tried.

When I got home that night, I wrote in my journal that if I ever wrote a book or chapter on healing, I would call it Jazz+Blueberries. Because, it was on that summer night, a night filled with the best jazz music in the park and Trader Joe's sweet blueberries that I realized something. We get to choose to love people. We get to choose to extend grace to one another. And, if God, who is perfect, has grace for us daily, how much more should we have grace for one another?

We all have chapters that we wish weren't part of our stories, but they are. A lot of us carry around a lot of wounds and hurts that were caused by other people, some of which only therapy can help heal. This is only a devotional and in just a few short words, I can't do a talk on mental health justice, but trust me when I say that if you are going through trauma, it is okay to get help. All the more, I think it is necessary to get help. I share more about this later on in the book, because therapy was a big part of my healing journey. Psalm 147:3 states, "He heals the brokenhearted and binds up their wounds." If your heart is broken today, if you have been wounded by a person or circumstance, there is hope, because Jesus came to heal the brokenhearted. More so, please understand that healing is a process. Don't try to rush through the process, because healing does take time. So, keep leaning on His strength, because one day, all the broken pieces will be restored. That's His promise, not mine.

No life is perfect. If we sat around at the dinner table together, we would all begin to realize something. Life is hard. But, with Jesus, it is a beautiful gift. Even on the days when we don't know what comes next, we can lift our gaze to set eyes on His and know that in the end, we are going to be okay. While we can't change the past, we can choose not to live in the past. We may look at our lives today and wish that there was something that we could change or looked different about today. You may not be able to change your reality, but you can change your today by choosing the right perspective. The right perspective changes everything.

As I sat in that park in Long Beach, there were so many things that I wished were different. I wished that this person I loved didn't have to battle with depression. I wished that I didn't come from a broken home. I wished that there was a way to erase the past and come up with a new narrative. And, while I could not change my reality, God showed something so beautiful to me. He told me to look up. So, that's exactly what I did. I looked up at the blue sky, I looked at the birds that flocked together in all their beauty, I looked at my blueberry stained fingertips, and then I looked at the smile on the face of this loved one, this broken person who is also a daughter of the King. Joy filled my lungs in such an inexpressible way. Jesus is beside us every moment of every day. What better hope is there than this? We aren't guaranteed tomorrow. We aren't guaranteed happiness. But, if we so choose, we are guaranteed life in Jesus Christ.

Today, I don't know what your world looks like. I don't know what pain you carry. I don't know what tomorrow holds. But, I do know this: God is faithful. We can show up with blueberry stained lips and sing off key together, while the haunting questions still stand in the back of our minds as to what will happen once the sweet music comes to an end. Even in the midst of our troubles, we can find peace in Him. Jesus came to tell you and I that one day, we can enjoy the goodness and sweetness of summertime again.

JENNIFER MALECH

29

ACCEPTING THE CALL

"You have been set apart and chosen for His purpose."
-Deuteronomy 14:2

In studying the major prophets of the Old Testament, I am simply astounded at the life that Jeremiah led. As we lead our own lives, I wonder what Jeremiah would think if he showed up to 21ˢᵗ century America. I wonder if he would ask us, "Do you understand what this is all about? Do you truly understand the call?" At times, Western Christianity doesn't always look like biblical Christianity. This is why studying the Scriptures is so important. It gives us true guidance for how we are meant to live our lives as Christians.

In this very familiar passage of scripture, Jeremiah 29:19 states, "For I know the thoughts that I think toward you, says the Lord, thoughts of peace and not of evil, to give you a future and a hope." Wow, this is such a beautiful promise! It's a verse that I have held onto many times throughout my life.

However, when we read the context of this verse and what it meant to Jeremiah's life, we might be at a loss for words. Instead of making you go do your research (although, you can go fact check me if you'd like), I'm going to give you some of the back story right now. Jeremiah was called by God when he was just about twenty-one years old. This is another reminder to us that age should never be a deterring factor in pursuing God's call on our lives. Jeremiah answered the call. Although, he wasn't quite convinced at first. In fact, he really didn't think he was qualified for the job.

"Then said I, "Ah, Lord God! Behold, I cannot speak, for I am a youth." But the Lord said to me: "Do not say, 'I am a youth,' For you shall go to all to whom I send you, And whatever I command you, you shall speak. Do not be afraid of their faces, for I am with you to deliver you" says the LORD." -Jeremiah 1:6-8. Wow. What an incredible call.

Chosen by God, the thoughts and plans that God had for Jeremiah's life was something that I'm quite certain none of us would be running to the front line, shouting, "Pick me! Pick me!" Simply put, we would not be eager to volunteer as tribute.

The more that you read about Jeremiah's life, the more you admire what he walked through to live out the calling God had placed on his life. In fact, Jeremiah led a very lonely life. He is often referred to as the weeping prophet. Have you ever read Lamentations? Yeah, he wrote that book. He never married or had a family to call his own. Talk about loneliness of immeasurable portions. As though the loneliness he faced wasn't enough, he had men who were plotting to kill him. Furthermore, he was mocked and seen as a laughing stock to the people of Judah. Jeremiah was an outcast.

Yet, despite all of this, God used Jeremiah in a mighty and powerful way to be a spokesperson for Him and His Kingdom. Through the difficulty, through the pain, through every lonely night, Jeremiah put his entire hope and future into the hands of God. Though the plans may have changed along the way, the expected end remained the same: one day, there would be restoration in Judah.

By no means does this mean that if we are to choose the call that God has placed on our lives that we will live a life of emotional and physical isolation, but rather, simply put, Jeremiah's life reveals that whatever difficult circumstances we may be facing in our own personal lives, God has a plan in it.

When you feel isolated and left out, especially when you are the only one in your family living for God, He will honor you for it. I know it can be hard at times. This Christian walk was never meant to be a walk in a park, so if you are new to all of this, please be reassured that when the difficult times come, you aren't missing something or doing something wrong. Life was never meant to be a walk in the park, for any of us. But, the wonderful hope is this: God is with us. When we choose to live for God, there is a good end. There is hope. At times, it may mean that we will have to go through lonely seasons so that we can celebrate the infinite hope that is found in Him. Matthew 22:14 states, "Many are called, but few are chosen."

Your calling is different from mine, and it is going to require a choice on your part that says, "Yes, LORD. I say yes to the uncomfortable and the less traveled road. No matter the cost, even if it is the cost of my own life, I will accept the invitation. I will answer the call." Jeremiah led an astounding life that sought the expected end: restoration to a nation buried in sin.

It can be difficult to understand the great length of sacrifice that many characters in the Bible took so that God's restoration and redemption could take place in entire nations. There are some things that God has called us into that requires great sacrifice. Anointing always requires sacrifice. If anything, Jeremiah's story reminds us that anointing comes with a cost. **Don't ever envy someone's anointing. You don't know what it cost them to get it.**

When our lives belong to Christ, we can be assured that God is using the darkest nights of our lives to turn them around to be the greatest light in someone else's story.

Before Jeremiah walked through his own trials, God promised him in Jeremiah 1:8, "Do not be afraid of their faces, for I am with you to deliver you." I am sure there were many times where Jeremiah began to doubt God and His plan, but He kept holding onto the promise, a promise that eventually led to the deliverance of an entire nation. This is such an incredible reminder to just keep walking in obedience to God's

Word. God will use this season for His greater purpose.

30

A GRANDFATHER'S NOTE

"Joseph had his prison, Daniel had his lion's den, David was hunted like an animal by Saul, yet all of these were in God's will and used by God."
-Henry Moore

During my Freshman year of college, I received letters from my grandfather. To this day, they are the most precious items that I own. The above quote was found in one of those letters that my grandfather had written to me just a year before he passed away. Just like Paul encouraged Timothy in his service to the Lord, my grandfather did the same for me. To anyone who knew Bro. Moore and his ministry, you know how much of a gift he was to the church. And, while he no longer walks this earth, his legacy lives on. I am so blessed to have books filled with his sermon notes, some dating all the way back to the 1950's when he first began his ministry, after graduating from Tupelo Bible Institute with his B.A. in Theology. I have taught many lessons from his sermons and teachings, and am so grateful for his wisdom that is still being imparted into my life today. It is for this reason that this entire book is dedicated to Henry A. Moore, a man whose dedication and sacrifice is one of the reasons I am here today.

One day, when I was in high school, as he sipped on a cup of coffee that was probably three days old, I read some of my writing to my grandfather. (We gave my grandmother the hardest time for heating up days old coffee. He never complained, but you better believe he drove down the street to McDonald's for a better cup of coffee. Oh, what a treasure their love was). As I read my writing to my grandfather, I watched as his eyes lit up. When I finished, he looked at me with a smile on his face and encouraged me to never stop writing. I will forever be grateful for his voice in my life.

My grandfather was a faithful man of God who made the greatest impact in my own spiritual life. His letters to me during my freshman year of college are some of the most treasured items I own. He taught me, from the moment I was old enough to understand, that life would not be easy; yet, if I learned to place my daily trust in God, His will would always take place in my life.

Through my grandfather's eloquent cursive, I found something so much deeper beyond the words he had just shared with me on paper. As I prepared one day to teach from these words that my grandfather had written, I was reminded that each of us will face our own prison and lion's den so to speak, yet it is up to us on what we will do once we are placed there. We can either let these seasons destroy us or let it give us direction towards God's higher calling. **If we recognize that we are in the perfect will of God and place our ultimate trust in His plan, which is higher than our ways, He will work all things together to be used by Him.** I shared this scripture previously, but I want to share it again.

> *"For my thoughts are not your thoughts*
> *Nor are your ways my ways," says the LORD*
> *For as the heavens are higher than the earth,*
> *So are my ways higher than your ways*

And My thoughts than your thoughts"
Isaiah 55:8-9

We have to believe that there is a greater purpose in all things and that God's ways are truly higher than our own. Romans 8:28 states, "And we know that all things work together for good to those who love God, to those who are the called according to His purpose."

In the LORD's prayer, it is mentioned, "Not my will, but yours be done." Sometimes, I believe we pray that prayer not realizing exactly what we are praying for and when the lion's den or prison cell comes our way, we immediately become frustrated and ask God, "Why? Why is this happening?" God doesn't ask for us to understand, He simply asks us to trust in Him and His plan. When we accept His will above our own, our perspective on our circumstances change. We will then begin to understand, just like Joseph, David, and Daniel had to come to understand, that our trust has to be in the One who knows beginning to end.

After my grandfather had graduated from Bible College, his first assignment was as an Associate Pastor at a church in Pasadena, CA. When he had arrived at the little church in Pasadena off Rosemead Ave, he felt very strongly that he wouldn't be staying for long as God was leading him elsewhere. And, he was right. Shortly after, he ended up pastoring in Turlock and South Gate before pastoring for 37 years in Salinas, California. What is crazy about this story is that exactly sixty years later from when he had left that Pasadena church, his granddaughter stepped foot in a church in Monrovia, CA. I didn't realize it at first, but it just so happened to be the same church that my grandfather had pastored at in Pasadena. The church had just moved to a different location. And, it is here, at this church that my grandfather first started his full-time ministry, that I was baptized in Jesus name and first stepped into the ministry myself. Seeds that were planted by my grandfather were reaped years later. We don't know why God calls us to certain places for a season, but I do believe there is a purpose. It is stories like this that remind me that God truly does care about every detail of our lives and spins it all together to create something masterful. I will forever be grateful for my grandfather's willingness to live a life in pursuit of God. Because of the decision he made all those years ago, his ministry lives on today.

MY TESTIMONY

"God uses broken things. It takes broken soil to produce a crop, broken clouds to give rain, broken bread to give strength. It is the broken alabaster box that gives forth perfume. It is Peter, weeping bitterly, who returns to greater power than ever."

-Vance Harver

Of everything you read in this book, this chapter was the hardest to write. I've asked God to guide my heart as I write and share with you all my story. I'm asking Him to show me how much to share and how much I should leave for conversation over coffee. I don't know who picked up this book, but I pray that if you have walked through any painful season of life, that this chapter is for you. May you find hope in knowing that we can surrender all the broken pieces over to Jesus. In fact, Jesus invites us to give our pain over to Him. Jesus endured the greatest of pain when He took the wounds to His back, the thorns in his skull, and piercings to his hands and feet, so that we could be made whole. It not only was so that we could receive salvation through His sacrifice, but so that through His wounds, we would also be able to experience emotional and physical healing in our lives, too.

As I was writing this book, I received a random message from someone I serve in ministry with who said, "People need to hear your story." I could almost hear my heart beat out of my chest as I read that text and felt confirmation in my spirit to share these words.

Revelation 12:11 states, "And they have defeated him by the blood of the Lamb and by their testimony." There is so much power in our stories, because our testimonies give voice to the power of redemption in our lives. Our stories bring into the light what the enemy meant to keep in darkness. I don't know your story, but I want to encourage you today. Never stop telling your story.

My hope is that as I share my story, you will feel encouraged to share yours, too. As I share these words, I know that there are others out there who have also walked a very similar road. Remember, whatever your story is, you are not alone. There are others out there who need to hear what you've been through, so that they may find hope, knowing that God is able to help anyone become an overcomer. Whatever situation you find yourself in today, it is not too difficult for Him.

Our stories bring hope, and it is hope that gives us the strength to keep on. I believe, no matter where you come from, if you surrender your life over to Him, Jesus will bring healing to your story. That's His promise. He came so that you and I wouldn't have to remain in brokenness, but so that we may find complete freedom in Christ. When I first received that text that I was supposed to share my story, I realized something. Just as this person already knew, I came to realize that God didn't carry me through all the pain so that I may remain silent about it, but He carried me to the other side so that I could give voice to the freedom that is found when we realize that we are overcomers through the blood of the Lamb.

Telling our stories makes us realize that we are not alone and helps us to point one another's toes towards heaven, towards the only hope that will bring restoration and healing back into the places that were once broken into a tiny million pieces. While I don't believe that God purposefully allows terrible things in our lives to happen, I do believe that God can take the most broken of situations and turn it around for His glory.

The reason why I think many of us don't share what we've been through is because we are afraid of what will happen when we do. And, let me tell you, that voice of fear is the enemy. He is trying to intimidate you and keep you in a state of fear so that you won't bring his schemes into the light. God has so much goodness planned for your life, and if you can push fear aside, I promise you that your voice can be a catalyst for so many people's lives.

Through a small glimpse into my world, I pray that God would reveal to you that no broken thing is wasted. I pray that my words may help someone out there who needs to be reminded that God is with you, every step of the way. I wish I could tell you why you had to endure what you went through, but I can't. The only thing I can tell you is that God is faithful, and no matter where you find yourself today, God wants to use your testimony for a greater purpose. So, here is a piece of my story.

Starting from the age of fourteen, there were various events that took place in my life that resulted in great emotional trauma. It affected both my physical and mental health in a very negative way and held me trapped in a lot of lies for years. The unfortunate part about emotional abuse is that when you are going through it, it is very difficult to function outside it. You feel as though you are trapped inside a cage of which there is no means of escape. And, then, as soon as it is over, you try to forget and convince yourself that everything is fine. You keep silent, because you are afraid of what will happen once you give voice to what has happened to you. So, instead of giving voice to it, you endure the pain until you just can't take it anymore.

The pain, at times, felt unbearable. I felt unsafe when I found myself in certain situations, and endured days that felt like a living nightmare that would never come to an end. I would go to work, school, and church with a smile on my face and try to forget the hours that had felt like a living nightmare.

When I was in high school, I would sometimes shut down emotionally around family and friends because I was having a hard time processing it all. During this time, I truly began to believe that I was the cause for everything dysfunctional that was happening around me. I felt worthless. At this point in my life, my relationship wasn't where it needed to be with Jesus, so I tried to find it in other places, whether it was in my drive for success to try to numb the pain or it was in activities that were far removed from Jesus. I felt so broken and confused. It was during my senior year of high school that I recommitted myself to Christ and began my journey towards healing. And, it is the best decision I ever made.

When I graduated from high school and moved seven hours outside the city I grew up in, it was for the best. It was during my college years that my pastors and a close friend who was a psychologist helped guide me through all of the emotional trauma that I had experienced since my teenage years. I found healing while I was in college, and thought that part of my story was over. After ten weeks of therapy and many nights of prayer, I was whole. I would never have to endure any of that ever again. But, unfortunately this was not the case. Emotional trauma became part of my story again. I can't put into words the pain that took place during those years. It was the foggiest season of my life. While I had experienced a lot of healing while I was in college, there were so many unaddressed issues that had been buried really deep. Like a bandage being ripped off a wound, all of the brokenness and pain became absolutely overwhelming.

I remember distinctly walking into church one day, and those who didn't know the situation would look me in the eyes and say, "Wow. You look so tired." I would gently laugh and come up with some story about work taking a toll on me. Afterwards, I remember sadly thinking, "If only it was work. Gosh, I wish it was work. Why couldn't it be the stress of work that was taking a toll on my life?" Work stress, I was experiencing that, too. But, work stress seemed like nothing in comparison to the pain that I was going through. In fact, I welcomed work stress, because it was a welcomed distraction from what I had to face once I left the office every day.

Needless to say, I was very broken. It wasn't until I crashed and totaled my car, due to the emotional strain of what had been happening in my life, that I realized God was trying to wake me up. I realized that if I didn't get help, then my life was headed in a very destructive direction. I had to get help. I couldn't keep trying to do this on my own. Thank God for His ultimate protection over my life that day.

I am so thankful to both my friends and my pastors who walked with me during that season, even when I was stubborn and tried to do things my own way. I am thankful for the therapists who helped give me the tools to know what to do in a very difficult position that I had been put in. The voices of spiritual authority and professional doctors helped give me the keys to walk through the emotional trauma and onto the other side. And, through it all, through all of the brokenness, I discovered a strength that I didn't even know was possible. My pain brought me to a new level in my relationship with Jesus. When I surrendered the broken pieces to Jesus, He didn't leave them on the ground. He began to piece them back together to make me whole again. **There was something about being completely broken that brought me to a new level in my relationship with Jesus.** I realized that if I wanted to experience true healing and restoration in my life, there were really difficult choices that I would have to make to live a life in true freedom. And, that journey started with forgiveness.

Sometimes, I look at my life and am simply amazed that not only am I alive today, but that I am healthy, both mentally and emotionally. In the process of becoming whole, God showed me that forgiveness and boundaries are an absolutely necessary part of our stories. Forgiveness isn't just about saying in your heart, "Okay, I forgive that person. It is done." It is much more. It is a conscious choice to leave the hurt and the pain at the foot of the cross and surrender that person over to Jesus. Alongside forgiveness, it is important to understand that boundaries are absolutely necessary towards a life of freedom.

Every situation is unique and while I can't lay out the specifics or really share with you the details of what happened in my own life, I want to use this space to gently tell you that it is so important to seek out both spiritual and professional help. Accountability in your life will be your saving grace. It is so important to seek out help. Don't try to do this on your own. Just like someone who is physically ill seeks a professional doctor for help in their healing process, it is important that those who have walked through emotional trauma seek out professional help through therapy. I also want to say to the man or woman who is so scared to speak to someone about what you have walked through, that I understand. It is okay to be scared, but it is also necessary that you seek help if you are to live a life of wholeness. Healing begins when we invite others into that journey and become vulnerable with others and ourselves. Ephesians 4:25 states, "Therefore, having put away falsehood, let each one of you speak the truth with his neighbor, for we are members of one another." You aren't meant to carry the pain on your own. That is the beauty of the church. It is a safe place to share with others what you have been through and invite others to pray alongside you as you find healing and restoration in Christ.

While God is absolutely capable of redeeming and healing your mind and emotions, I am a firm believer that God also put therapists here on this earth to help give humans the tools to help us through the mental thought patterns that we have found ourselves trapped in. I am also here to say that God is able to take away all the shame, the guilt, the fear, and the lies that any of us have believed for too long. God loves us too much to leave us where He found us. On the night when I was the most broken, God wrapped me up in His love in a way that cannot be found through anything or anyone else on this earth.

When it came to my own journey towards complete healing, I had to set up boundaries in my life. At the end of the day, you will have to be the one who will have to make the tough decision to build those boundaries with others. It's called tough love. And, let me tell you, it hurts. But, it is absolutely necessary if you are to have healthy relationships with other people in your life. No matter the various kinds of relationships that exist in our life, it is important to understand that boundaries are necessary. God will give you strength and wisdom to make your way through those tough decisions. When healthy boundaries are put in place, we can still love the broken people in our lives. I know there are some really good books out there on the subject of boundaries, but I am not going to try to write about all of that here. One, because I don't consider myself an expert and two, it would take the rest of our time together. So, instead, I just want to share this: **Boundaries in your relationships may be the very thing that will protect your life and ministry.**

My friend Charity reminded me, "Until others let go of their own burdens, no reconciliation will be lasting." If you are seeking reconciliation in a relationship, understand that you can find peace for yourself when you forgive and give your burdens over to the Lord, but you cannot force someone else to forgive or release their own burdens of the past. I had to learn that I cannot change the people I love, especially those who have hurt me. Only God can do that. There are some circumstances that are outside our own control. There is freedom when you understand this and release other people into the hands of God, rather than taking it into your own hands. Today, I live in freedom. I no longer respond as a victim, but I respond as a victor who knows that no person on this earth can have power over me and my emotions.

While life may not be perfect (it never will be while we are here on earth), our lives are made whole and perfect in Christ. In the past few years, God has done so much healing in my heart and mind that I didn't even know was possible. He has brought reconciliation into the relationships that were once broken. The subject of reconciliation, oh my. That would require another book altogether. Today, I have peace, knowing that every broken piece and every person in our lives can be surrendered over to Christ. We are broken people loving broken people, put back together by a perfect God. Healing is an ongoing process, and through it all, God has shown me that no matter who you are, no matter your story, wholeness is possible.

There is so much that God has done that I could not do on my own, so many hurts from my youth that have been uprooted and are now no longer taking root for unwanted things in my life. Through the process, God gave me a greater understanding about Him that I wouldn't have learned otherwise. He gave me a new perspective on life, showed me how to have compassion for others and how to better love the broken people in my own life. Because of Jesus, there is a love overflowing in my heart for those who, at times, were the cause of great emotional pain. What I realized, at the end of it all, is that the people who had hurt me were loving me to the best of their abilities, through their own brokenness, depression, anger, etc. When they, too, realized they were in the wrong and asked for forgiveness, I was able to offer it simply because Jesus had forgiven me, too.

God is asking us to surrender all of our brokenness and burdens over to Him. Psalm 55:22 states, "Cast your burden on the Lord, and He shall sustain you; He shall never permit the righteous to be moved." When we continually look to God in the midst of our trials and surrender our lives over to Him, we can be assured that He will use us in the midst of it all. As we walk through the foggy seasons, He will sustain us.

Jesus endured brokenness at the cross. Yet, the story did not end there. His resurrection tells the greatest story of sacrifice. Without His brokenness, there would have been no story of redemption, and without redemption, we would have never been given access to the gift of the Holy Spirit. Wow.

You might be trying to understand how you will ever be made whole again. God will not only heal you, but God will use your story to reveal His glory. When you give your life to Christ and surrender to His will, I promise you that God is able to take every broken thing and turn it around for His good. It is because of the brokenness that I endured that this book came to be. I am so thankful for the grace of God that held me and carried me through every dark chapter, so that I could write this book. What a powerful truth it is, to know that God can redeem the most broken of situations and turn it into something far more beautiful than what the enemy tries to steal from us.

The love of Jesus is the one thing that has carried me through every painful circumstance. God was with me through it all, even on the darkest night. And, now, He has begun to take every piece of my life and use it for His glory. The painful chapters of our stories reveal the power of God's redemption all the more. That's God promise, not mine.

While this is only a glimpse of my story, because ten years cannot be captured in a short devotional, I will tell you that God was so faithful through it all. You may be praying for a situation that is outside your own control right now, and let me tell you this, God is still in it. God has never left your side. It is on the darkest night that I learned to see the light in a whole new way. God's light is revealed all the more powerfully in the darkness. It is when my prayers felt unheard that God reminded me to just be still, to stop trying to figure things out on my own and to lean into His strength. God never intended for us to live in bondage, but He will use the seasons that held us captive for something so much greater than what meets the eye. God created you to live in freedom, and that freedom starts in your heart, when you surrender every broken thing over to Him. Restoration and healing is possible, no matter how far away that possibility seems today.

Trauma is very real in our day and age today, and if you are someone who has had to walk through physical or emotional trauma, I want to be the first to say I am so sorry you had to go through that. I am so sorry that your mind or body was abused, and that you are the victim who now carries around those wounds. But, I am also here to say that there is hope. God wants to do a miracle in your life. He will cover up the wounds and leave a scar that will scream louder than the emotions that had you buried in so much pain. God will use your scars. When Jesus resurrected, He could have returned in an unscathed body, but instead, He kept the scars. He kept the scars as a testament to the power of who He is. In the same way, our scars will be used to reveal redemption found through Him alone.

Last night, as I was going through an old journal of mine, I found a two-line entry that I had written exactly a year ago, to the day. "The enemy wants nothing more than for you to stop writing. Don't ever stop telling your story."

So, today, I shared a small piece of my story, to remind the enemy of his place. Because he can try ever tactic under the sun, but nothing on this earth can separate us from God's love and redemption plan. You may not be ready to share any part of your testimony yet, and that's okay. But, I promise you that God will use every part of your story if you surrender it over to Him. I kept things very vague out of respect for other parties involved, but wanted to shed light on the fact that no matter what kind of experiences you have had to face in this life, there is hope in Jesus. There is so much that I left unwritten because there are some things in our life that aren't meant for the whole world to know. We aren't meant to share everything with everyone, but if there are pieces of your story that will help someone else mend, listen to the Holy Spirit when you feel that gentle nudge to open up.

I wrote this chapter to let you and I know that God is the Author of my story. God is the Author of your story. I promise you, if you let Him, He will use your story to make an impact in ways that you could have never predicted. Surrender everything over to Him. Giving our lives to Jesus is the best decision we could ever make. He is making something beautiful out of the broken pieces. This is not the end.

CONCLUSION

"If you forget that God's plan for your life is to grow, you'll become frustrated with your circumstances. There are some things that you will learn about God through suffering that you wouldn't have been able to learn any other way. Your circumstance you are facing is your temporary, but your character is eternal."
-Pastor Rich Brown

I wanted to end this book with a quote from my Pastor, whose teaching has had a great impact on my life. I call it steak and potatoes teaching, because every lesson that he has taught is so rich, ha! (Did you catch the pun?)

Over the years, I have collected so many notes from his teachings. And, while I could fill up this entire book with lessons that I have learned under his leadership, this particular quote really stood out to me, especially with the theme found in this book. It is safe to say that there are things that we will learn about God through suffering that we wouldn't be able to learn any other way.

The circumstances we are facing are temporary and so small in comparison to what eternity has in store for us. I want to end this book with where we started. I also think this is about the third or fourth time that I have shared this verse. As I said, if this book was given a theme verse it would be 2 Corinthians 4:17-18. "For our light affliction, which is but for a moment, is working for us a far more exceeding *and* eternal weight of glory, while we do not look at the things which are seen, but at the things which are not seen. For the things which are seen *are* temporary, but the things which are not seen *are* eternal."

Through every foggy morning, may we be reminded that seeds are being planted. **Your today may not make sense to you, but your tomorrow depends on today's attitude.** When you choose to turn and shift your attention towards heaven, you can find peace in knowing that God is walking alongside you every step of the way. To choose an attitude of gratitude, even in the mist of the pain, is to have a posture of strength that will carry you through every season of life.

It is in the lonely and foggy seasons of life that we find God in a way that we wouldn't have otherwise. A deeper relationship with God is being birthed and I promise you that when you make it to the other side, you will be so grateful. We can't always feel or understand what God is doing, but one day, we will look back and see just how faithful God has been during each trial and circumstance of our lives. We are humbled in these seasons, and we are reminded that our lives are but a mere vapor to which we know that this world is not our home. We are only passing through.

On March 9 this past year, I had just gone through one of the most difficult 24 hours of my life. I forced myself to go to a coffee shoppe and read from Lysa Terkeurst's book, *It's Not Supposed to Be This Way*. It was seven in the morning, and as my body tried to warm up with a cup of coffee I was slowly sipping on, Lysa's words spoke directly to my situation.

"If God gave out Purple Hearts, you would absolutely receive this high honor. What you are going through won't be for nothing. Your hurt will not be wasted. It will be for the saving of many lives…God isn't far off. He's just far more interested in your being prepared than in your being comfortable. God will take every cry you've uttered and arrange those sounds into a glorious song. He will add it to His symphony of compassion. You will have a starring solo in which those notes birthed from tears will ease the ache of another…Close your eyes and breathe. You're brave. A decorated soldier in this horrible battle with a glorious ending."

As I fought back the tears in that coffee shoppe, I knew in the depth of my heart that God knew what He was doing. Through the most difficult of circumstances, He was teaching me how to pick up my sword and fight. I knew that no matter what happened next, this certainly was not the end.

Since that day, the miracle I was searching for did eventually come, and in the process, I discovered that God was writing my story so that I could share it with others, and point others to the hope we have when we place our full trust in Him.

I know that throughout my life, there will be more trials to come, and when I can't find my way through the fog, I will need to read these words again. I believe that when we surrender our lives to Christ, no hurt will be wasted. Our lives are in His hands. We have the choice. Will we choose to depend on our own strength or will we choose to trust in Him?

"When you pass through the waters, I will be with you; and through the rivers, they shall not overwhelm you; when you walk through the fire you shall not be burned, and the flame shall not consume you. For I am the LORD your God."
                                                                -Isaiah 42:3-4

I am full of gratitude today, that even though I want the answer to "the why" questions, those answers are not mine to hold. But, this I do know, our stories will be a beacon of light to those who need it most. There is no greater joy than to walk with the LORD. There is nothing sweeter than to know Him. With joy in my heart, I want to let you know that your story will be turned into God's glorious song. No foggy morning goes without His notice.

While I hope this book has been a comfort, I want to remind you and I to insert ourselves daily into the Word of God. Our daily relationship with God is the most important part of our lives. Stories are important, because they remind us that we are not alone. But, no story can replace the Word of God in your life. It is the greatest storybook every written. From Genesis to Revelation, it is God's love letter to us. In reading His Word, we will discover His heartbeat, we will learn how we must live our lives, and we will continually be guided into the light, when other voices try to deter us away from it. The Word is our foundation. Without it, we won't ever get to know God in the way He intended for us to truly know Him. **Plant yourself in His Word and watch as He changes your life in the most beautiful and unexpected ways.** There is no better way to start your day. God's Word will bring peace on the foggiest of mornings and help lead you and I home.

FINAL THOUGHTS & ACKNOWLEDGEMENTS

Thank you. Thank you so much for picking up this book and adding it to your shelf. Thank you for reading these words and going on this journey with me. I pray that in some way God spoke to you through one of the devotionals found in this book. It was my honor to write this book and I am so blessed beyond measure to have shared God's heartbeat with you all. I hope that during this time together, you have been encouraged and strengthened in your own personal walk with God. Our God is fighting for us. There is a church that is supporting you and praying alongside you. May we continually use our gifts to encourage one another and point one another's toes towards heaven.

When I first started gathering these pieces of my heart on paper, I asked God to let His Holy Spirit lead me in the words He wanted me to share with this generation. I didn't want to just write what I thought would be best, which is why this book went through a lot of editing and revisions. I deleted entire entries and went back to the drawing board, asking that God would reveal His heartbeat. In the last hours before the final draft of this book was submitted, I almost deleted my testimony from the book altogether. But, God's voice kept whispering in my ear, "Tell your story." Because, this is what I do know: My story isn't just mine, but it is many others, too.

Even if our stories read differently, you and I are very similar. We are able to relate to one another because we have all faced the same emotions, the same questions, the same heartbreak, the same doubts. While there are a lot of questions that I still have, many of which will never be answered this side of heaven, I wrote the words in this book so that we could be reminded that no pain is wasted when we surrender it back into the arms of our Heavenly Father.

I pray, more than ever, that we would be a church who live in unity with one another. I pray that we would not live a life of comparison and would continually become others focused in our day to day living. We are the church. It is by our love for one another that others will come to know Jesus. It starts in the church. May that all-consuming love spread into our homes, our communities, and our cities. May we use our own stories to point others to the hope of the cross. Keep walking with Him, no matter what comes your way, because the pain will lead you and others to His love. I am so grateful and overwhelmed that God trusts us enough to take us through the foggy mornings so that we may know how to better praise Him in the sunshine.

I shared in an interview a couple years ago that through my writing, this is the message that I want to share with others, "If everything was stripped away from you, would you still be able to say God is enough? At times, I probably wouldn't be able to say that. But, in the dark seasons of life, when He's all you have, you realize, "Alright. He is enough." We have to get to that place. I want to see our generation get ahold of that: God is enough. That is what this past year for me has been all about. In my most difficult season, Jesus you are enough. I've never been more intimate with God or found more supernatural joy in all my life."

There is something so powerful and beautiful when you discover the supernatural joy of God. It becomes contagious, and you can't help but want to share it with others. I pray that through the stories found in this book, you were reminded of the love and inexpressible joy that we get to experience when we live for God.

This book, of course, would not have been possible without the encouragement, guidance, support and love from some incredible friends and mentors in my life.

First, to my pastor and his wife, Rich and Tamara Brown, thank you for pouring into me over these past seven years. You have both taught me what it means to live a life that is bought out to the Truth and have encouraged me to live a life that is daily on mission for His purpose. Thank you for walking alongside me during the rough patches, pointing me in the right direction, and for welcoming me into your family with open arms.

To my spiritual mentor and friend, Stephanie Guzman (better known as Mama G), I can never thank you enough. You have fasted and prayed with me and have truly been a pillar of faith in my life. You are one of the strongest women I know, and I am forever grateful that God placed you and your family in my life. And, of course, thank you for making sure I was always fully stocked on oatmeal when my kitchen pantry was bare. You are the best.

To my friends, Charity Hall and Drew Keatts, thank you for your daily encouragement. You were the first two people who bought the e-book version of Through the Morning Fog all those years ago and told me to get this book on paper. When I first decided to re-write this book, you cheered me on and supported me every step of the way.

To my friends, Sarah Winkle, Amy Colwell, and Starr Garcia, thank you for walking with me through the really rough patches, and welcoming me into your homes when I needed a place to stay. You guys are the true definition of friends who love selflessly and provide support in the best possible ways.

And, to my friends Samantha Solovieff and Lauren Sadler, thank you. Although there is distance that separates us in miles, you both are always so close to me. You have both been here with me, every step of the way. Thank you for every phone call, text message, and wise word that gave me strength on the hardest of days. And, Sam, thank you for being a real champ when I lost my cool in England. I enjoyed re-telling that story in this book.

To my friend, Caymbria Brown, I am so grateful for your friendship, for always supplying our lives with puns and for being a constant joy in my life. You are wise beyond your years and I can't wait to see what the future holds. Lastly, I would like to thank my brother, Josh Malech, for being by my side through the thick of it, and for letting me use one of his photographs for an epic cover for this book. It turned out better than I could have hoped! You inspire me in so many ways. Thank you for serving our country and blessing so many people's lives with your sacrifice.

The list could go on and on as I am truly blessed with the most wonderful of friends and a church family that has continually encouraged me in my writing. This book is for all of you.

THROUGH THE MORNING FOG

REFERENCES

Chan, Francis. (2008). Crazy Love: Overwhelmed by a Relentless God.

Chambers, Oswald. (1935). My Utmost for His Highest.

Lewis, C.S. (1952). Mere Christianity

Lewis, C.S. (1940). The Problem of Pain

Miller, Donald. (2009). A Million Miles in a Thousand Years.

Terkeurst, Lysa. (2018). It's Not Supposed to Be This Way.

Thomas Nelson Bibles. (1982). The New King James Bible.

Tozer, A.W. (1948). The Pursuit of God.

Zondervan New International Version Faith in Action Study Bible (2011). General Author Terry C. Muck

THROUGH THE MORNING FOG

Made in the USA
Columbia, SC
18 March 2021